BOOKS BY

NAN FAIRBROTHER

The Cheerful Day *(1960)*

Men and Gardens *(1956)*

An English Year *(1954)*

THESE ARE

BORZOI BOOKS,

PUBLISHED IN NEW YORK BY

ALFRED A. KNOPF

THE
HOUSE
IN THE
COUNTRY

THE
HOUSE
IN THE
COUNTRY

NAN
FAIRBROTHER

NEW YORK
ALFRED A. KNOPF
MCMLXV

L. C. catalog card number: 65-11120

THIS IS A BORZOI BOOK,
PUBLISHED BY ALFRED A. KNOPF, INC.

FIRST AMERICAN EDITION

TO

WILLIAM

In the Country

CONTENTS

PART ONE

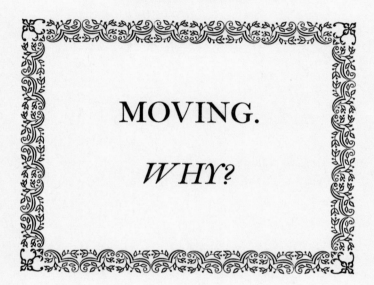

MOVING.

WHY?

1

IT WAS AN UNEASY WINTER. THE START OF AN earthquake. A long domestic upheaval which began with an almost imperceptible disquiet, grew to a climax which brought forth a house, then died away again nearly three years later to the normal rhythm of living.

The winter began like any other, settling in at the end of autumn against the months of cold and dark ahead, the annual sense of semi-hibernation with life snugly contracted into warm enclosures. Up till the shortest days it was a winter like any other, the dark half of the year's accustomed circuit, the night to summer's day.

The change began almost unnoticed at the turn of the year, no more at first than a vague indefinable restlessness, a disorientation of the inward-looking living of winter, as squirrels rouse from sleep and look about them in spells of mild weather. But as the days lengthen, the restlessness has grown with the growing daylight. It is a new and unaccountable disturbance. Not the familiar bored impatience of a too-long winter, nor even the moody discontent of spring which is the personality's change of season. These we recognize and accept as the yearly cycles of our emotional climate. But this is a restlessness both more diffuse and more particular. This, so I begin to realize, is a self-generated disturbance, no surface reaction to passing seasons but a shifting of the unseen foundations of living, the approach of one of the metamorphoses which mark the stages of human lives like the acts of a play.

Not that it troubles the rest of the family. Not in the least. The ground is not stirring beneath their feet as it is beneath mine. This beginning is my own personal earthquake, and their cheerful unconsciousness of my unsettled state sets them apart from the upheaval I am undergoing on their behalf as well as my own.

Domestic life is as usual: four of us living in the middle of London, two half-grown boys with their parents, William a doctor, the boys at day-school, all of us living comfortably together in a house we share with the doctor's practice. We are peaceful except for the changeable weather of adolescence, settled for years in the same well-run-in household, the daily, weekly, yearly routine of living long ago established. The boys rush off late for school in the mornings and saunter back full of news in the evenings, William is all day in and out between hospitals and patients. This winter like every other. Nothing is different. It is colder perhaps—and will there be skating for the boys in Regent's Park? And shall William rearrange his working week, he wonders, to see patients on different days? And my attack of flu takes longer to get over than usual. But nothing is different. Mere surface variations on the steady theme of our London life. But within the solid framework I am no longer steady.

When swallows grow restless to leave at the end of summer it is not for conscious reasons like colder weather or shortage of flies, but because the changing light of autumn disturbs the sensitive balance of their summer lives. And I too grow restless, not because our life is any less satisfactory (the weather is as warm as ever, the flies as plentiful) but only because the light is differ-

ent outside the window. It will soon be autumn. William and I
are in our forties, we begin to be middle-aged.

By a hundred questionings and discontents I begin to understand my restlessness. For since it is women who make the
domestic setting for families to live in, the periodic changes in a
household are brought about by a change in the settled condition of the housewife who runs it. And now, it seems, our family
life has reached a stage where it needs something done. It needs
rehousing. And my restless state is a growing consciousness that
I must rearrange our domestic affairs before I can settle down
again to the ordinary rhythm.

It is not simply that we need a different house—larger or
smaller or in a new place. What we need is a different basis of
living. It is no longer enough that the house we inhabit should be
a convenient accommodation for our working and family life.
Now that the season is changing outside our middle-aged windows, we need a settled base which we can think of as our fixed
family centre for as far ahead as we like to look. And this house
is not like that. It is not ours. We rent it from a landlord as a
convenient central lodging for two schoolboys and a London
doctor, and it has suited us excellently for years, combining our
working and private lives with generous urbanity. But it is not
ours, and though it may be long-term it is nonetheless temporary. We live in it always knowing we must leave, planning our
occupation from lease to lease renewed, and growing no permanent roots. As the sole anchor of our domesticity it will not do
any longer, and it is this growing awareness of our rootless living
which disturbs my winter peace.

That it does not disturb the rest of the family is nothing to
do with the matter. Naturally it does not, since domestically I
am their anchor, not the house, and for all they can tell I am still
as solid as I ever was. It would never occur to any of them that a
settled house was of any particular importance. Home is where
they come back to, and as far as they are concerned it exists

automatically because I run a house and they come back to it. And so perhaps it does with the perfect housewives. There may be archetypal women who simply by sitting in a strange room can create a home for a family. If so I have never met them (they are probably twin sisters of that equally rare species the Golden-hearted Prostitute) and certainly I am not one of them. I am not a solid enough rock to support a household unless I am solidly housed to begin with. I belong to the ordinary run of women with an instinct to make homes as birds make nests, but I need a settled place to do it. The nest-building instinct is strong in most women, and in pregnant mothers overwhelming. For the elaborate nurseries of pregnancy are for the pleasure of mothers, not for the blind oblivious baby whose whole world will be his mother's lap.

But William and I need no nurseries. Our children are fledged now and will soon leave the family nest. Our settled base will not be a harbour for young children but for their middle-aged parents. Of course there are the hypothetical future generations of family, but even though our increasingly precocious sons may soon start to shave in their cradles, I still find it hard to plan seriously for the future offspring of boys not yet even concerned with girl-friends, but only with passing O-levels. For us then. For William and me to settle in and the boys to come and go as they please.

As a family we are not conventionally united. We are none of us domestic enough for the birds-in-a-nest-agreeing atmosphere of hobbies shared and evenings round the communal hearth. To anyone used to a close family circle our domestic arrangements would seem uneasily draughty. But they suit us. For we each live a separate life with individual intensity, with different interests and friends, and quite independent arrangements. As a family we are four separate people who live under the same roof, and meet for an evening meal and the eager exchange of news of each other's affairs. Whatever the underlying bonds, our obvious everyday contact is interest and amusement. We none of us ever bore each other.

On the surface we are not noticeably affectionate, but families may be united in other ways than in a close domestic circle, and despite our individual independence our family force is surprisingly centripetal. We all come back. When we go off on our separate affairs we take with us the consciousness of the base we belong to. It is what others notice who meet us away from home—that we all belong where we come from. And though we go off constantly on our individual expeditions, we generally come back early. Indeed, we seldom stay away even a holiday to the end, and it has become one of the family amusements to make bets on how many days earlier than arranged any absent member will come home again. Sometimes we simply arrive on the doorstep with a carefully casual air of always intending to come back on Tuesday instead of Wednesday. Sometimes we are frankly unrepentant. "I went to the station to buy a paper and there was a train going to London. And I thought of you all doing things here without me, and I couldn't resist it. They put my bicycle in the guard's-van and here I am." A beaming smile.

So far the record for early returns is a week in advance, which even by our tolerant standards is surprisingly early, and all the three stay-at-homes lost their bets on the likely date for return. For the boys and I sat one night drinking coffee at our evening leisure and exchanging the news of our three separate days. The telephone rang. Could I take a personal call from France? Yes, I could—straightaway—but with dreadful misgivings, for we are none of us cosmopolitans to ring each other up with the Channel between us except in emergencies.

Then a faint but most reassuringly cheerful voice.

"How are you all? Yes. Of *course* I'm all right." (A surprised voice now.) "Yes. Perfectly all right. But I'm *not* ringing you up from the South of France. I'm *not* in Montpellier, I'm in Calais. But I'm having to spend the night here because the ferry can't take the car till tomorrow, so I thought I'd ring you up to explain."

To explain the *delay*, so the voice implied, and I suppose when we once decide for home, it can logically count as delay to arrive only seven days early instead of eight.

So one thing is clear, we need a common family centre for our separately revolving orbits, a base to be tethered to when we go abroad.

Very well. We need rehousing. And since the others are as unconcerned with such fundamentals of living as the dwellers at the top of a house are unconcerned with its foundations, I am the one who must rouse myself and achieve it.

Most of anyone's life is a preoccupation with urgent inessentials. If we divide our affairs into what matters for a day or a season or the rest of our lives, it is the long-term fundamentals we give least time to, and put off till tomorrow's tomorrow. We are more concerned with the pressing than the important, and the essentials are easily crowded out by the mere day-to-day business of living. After all, the business is far more amusing. Who would not rather choose new wall-paper for the living-room than worry about inadequate foundations?

But every so often we stand apart from our life and assess it as a whole. It may be a reappraisal inspired by outside change, by trouble or illness, or perhaps by some sudden realization of life running out. But not always. For me it is a mood of detached reassessment which haunts any long journey I make alone. Cut off from the preoccupations which enclose me at either end, I see my life from a judging distance. It is a salutary vision mostly, and much to be recommended as a cure for groundless discontent. For in the shelter of a happy life we grow over-exigent, and minor woes unduly disturb our cosseted state, but when judged by the harsher standards of the world in general, they shrink to their proper proportion. And perhaps the vision is always salutary, even for the truly wretched. For if a happy life looks brighter against the common shadowy background, a sad one may seem less inevitable. There are miseries we suffer from habit or inertia, or simply that in our shortsighted state we have not seen how to avoid them. A great many lives must have been rearranged on lonely journeys, and railway seats have probably inspired more understanding than all the psychiatrists' couches.

But I have no need of either journeys or troubles. For me the reassessment is a periodic and inescapable overhauling, like digging up a plant every so often to examine its roots. And this winter, however thriving the visible plant may be, its roots need repotting for the future. William and I are half-way through our lives and we still have no settled home. It is a fact. A frivolous and selfish and utterly unimportant fact.

◇◇◇◇ 2 ◇◇◇◇

I realize perfectly well that as a serious misfortune our unanchored state ranks with the Princess's pea. But then no one has ever suggested that the pea did not genuinely trouble that excessively fussy young woman. Within reasonable limits our emotional reaction also adjusts itself to the outside stimulus of life's peas, and that we have no real troubles seem only, alas, to make us over-sensitive to the more nebulous misfortunes, to the lumps under fifty mattresses. Besides, different species suffer different woes, and no one can judge for another. People are like trees in this business of changing house, there are good and bad movers, and I am one of the worst. I can only envy the fortunates who move from place to place with scarcely more ado than changing hotels on a journey. They seem born with a nautral gift for transplanting their lives, as self-contained as the rhododendrons at flower-shows, with their roots closely knit and rounded off in a net of sacking. They can move from house to house—from town to town even—and carry their essential life with them, rooting at once into any new soil. They suffer no sense of being wrenched from the setting which sustains them, as I do. They are stimulated, not dismayed, by the thought of leaving their own country, and exile would never for them be the bitter punishment it was for the Chinese and would be for me. They are no doubt the true inhabitants of our new mobile civilization, an enviable race with the whole world for home, and an inborn immunity to my anguished sense of not belonging.

When I was a child I had a recurrent desire which I still most vividly remember. I wanted to live in a place where a yew-hedge had been planted at my birth, and to watch it grow up year by year as I did. It is one of the few childhood desires which has kept its virtue, for most of them lose their appeal long before we are old enough to satsify them (like my greedy passion for evaporated milk, which I would drink down in gallons like water, so I promised myself, as soon as I was old enough to do as I liked).

But the yew-hedge I still understand, even though it is no longer what I sigh for, caring always more for the future than the past. And it was in place of my unattainable yew-hedge, I suppose, that every year of my growing-up I planted out the cast-off Christmas-tree when we turned out the Christmas decorations, wretched maltreated creatures which seldom made any attempt to survive; and when they did—took tentative root in our patch of poor city soil, and put forth diffident yellowish shoots from spring to spring—even then I could never stay to watch them grow to trees, but left them forlornly behind in the periodic removals of our normal nomadic twentieth-century family life.

Our childhood memories are vivid as nothing ever is again. So we are constantly told by poets and psychologists and everyone else. It is an article of modern post-Freudian faith, and never seriously questioned. But how far is it true for everyone, I wonder? Of course our childhood memories are vivid, otherwise we should not remember them. It is only because of their intensity that they survive at all from that largely forgotten far-off time so little registered by our conscious memory. And the things we remember from our childhood were imprinted on our consciousness, not because they were important in themselves but because for some reason we felt them vividly. They were important to our emotional life not to our intelligence, and we therefore still remember them with feeling. For our emotions change less than our intelligence from child to adult, and our memories therefore keep their significance because they are emotionally valid.

But, still, is it true for most people that after childhood we never again remember things with the same intensity? Certainly it is not true for me. Not only my childhood but all my life is scattered with memories intense and significant in just the same way. There is no break, no difference in kind. They are moments of vivid awareness which stamp the occasion unfading on my mind. An anonymous scene from remote childhood, a scene I can place exactly from a year ago and revisit tomorrow if I choose—there is no difference. They both belong equally in a landscape of memory irradiated by some special light of feeling —of pleasure mostly, delight in some beauty keenly felt then as now.

And among the remembered places are houses we have lived in, rooted in I suppose, but certainly remembered in a way as different from ordinary recollection as poetry is different from prose. There was one house especially, an old farmhouse where the children grew up in the country in a wartime world of our own, curiously remote and isolated. The house was beautiful certainly, and our life there must often have been reasonably happy despite the separations and boredoms and despairs of war. But looking back in memory the house shines with an astonishing beauty, which can only partly belong to everyday walls and a roof. Our remembered lives there have a curious enchanted feeling, isolated not only in time and place but in emotion. It is part of the poetry of memory, as a love-affair may be, or some exactly fortunate visit, or more often some trivial episode distinguished only by our remembering. For it is we who create the virtue, and the light shines from our own eyes, not from any outside sun. When we see them as the world does, our enchanted islands of experience change to mere ordinary plots, and even our farmhouse can fade to shabby mediocrity sheltering a workaday life.

For I visited it again a year or so ago. Passing one day down the old accustomed lane, I turned in at the gate and on through the orchard. But an everyday lane now, a commonplace orchard; mere skeleton statements of the enchanted leafy bowers I remembered. And the house? I stood in cold dismay to find it in the end so ordinary, so utterly disenchanted. Dead daffodils are not more changed from the living flowers than this drab building from the house I remember. It was as if a stage-set I had always seen richly illuminated by coloured lights were suddenly shown poor and mean in the grey revealing daylight. It was one of the stages of growing older. Older and sad.

I have always known that for other people my swans were geese, and it does not matter. But for me I thought they were swans immutably. Now I know they are not, and it matters profoundly. For I thought the magic was built into the house and would always be there: that I could come back from my different life and find it again whenever I chose. But although the transformation of geese to swans may not be a process limited to childhood, yet neither is it, as I supposed it was, a once-and-for-all metamorphosis. Instead it is a continuing activity of our emotional living and needs continuous energy; like holding up a weight against gravity or lighting a bulb with an electric charge. It is a reversible transformation, and is why we revisit the setting of our childhood at peril of disillusion.

But if the light fades when we leave it? And if the places we inhabit live only with a life borrowed from ours? Do we waste our substance by leaving anything we love, and risk our treasure on the high seas even by living away from it? As we grow older, shall we always be able to generate the transforming charge, or will there be no more radiant swans, but all future houses be bricks and mortar merely?

Or is this only mid-winter dumps? The cold, and being too much indoors? And if I went out and bought a new hat (that routine prescription for women's woes), should I feel no end better?

But who buys hats in January? Besides, buying hats is for me much like going to the dentist or having my photograph taken. I want a new house not a new hat. For if we cease in time to grow roots to sustain our lives in new places, then we must make sure of the rooting while we are still in the actively growing stage of existence. For the time may come when we are past any true transplanting, but only move about like trees in tubs set down in new places and never belonging.

Somewhere in Proust there is a passage where he describes his sorrow at finding he is no longer in love. To the young it is an inexplicable sadness. I still remember. Why should he grieve when the world is full of people to fall in love with, and new love always promises more than the old? But the promise is not in the other people, it is in ourselves. Encounters are only intensified to love-affairs by the force of our own vitality, and that is not inexhaustible. We shall outlive the emotional energy to project the magic over and over. For falling in love is an act of creation by the lover, and, far more than parting, to fall out of love is to die a little. We shall not always fall in love again—with other faces, other houses, other ways of living.

So I warn myself in the winter dusk with the London traffic streaming past the window.

But then the boys clatter in from school, overflowing with gossip and news of the town, and of how perishingly cold it was rowing on the river, and how can you tell if you've got frost-

bite *before* your toes drop off? And William comes in with a
rush, and asks have I remembered that we're going to the theatre,
and need to have supper early?

And the urgent crowds out the essential. But only as a passing
wind destroys a reflection on the surface of a pool. In the following quiet the reflection is there again; we must still move
house.

It is not that we can live in a new house yet. There are years
ahead of London working-life and the boys still half at home.
But we must find a house where we can settle and belong, where
we can grow into some particular place and way of living.
Whether we live there seven days a week or only one will make
no difference; we shall be safely rooted and no more transplanting. Our lives will be defined at last by steadily growing emotional yew-hedges.

◇◇◇◇ *3* ◇◇◇◇

To live in London and read Walpole's letters.

To live in the country and read White's *Selborne*.

Which?

Which do we want for a house of our own? It is not a new
question. On the contrary it is a question most Londoners consider at regular intervals. Where shall they live when they can
choose? Shall they move out to Blackheath and a garden? Or a
two-roomed flat conveniently in the centre? Or a cottage in
Devon or in country near London for week-ends? For city life
is not settled: it is swift and restless with probabilities of change.
Work may decide the base for our working lives, but where shall
we live when we are free to choose?

By middle-age we should know ourselves well enough to

· 14 ·

realize which are the pleasures that suit us, and to plan our lives reliably in terms of our own particular satisfactions. But so far only one thing is clear about the house William and I want—we must settle in it for good. It must be our last. And since the settled-for-good implies William's far-distant retirement it is no good choosing to suit present whims: we must try to foresee what we shall want in twenty years' time.

Though admittedly at this early stage it might be more accurate to describe it as the house *I* want, since the family are perfectly content where they are and still cheerfully blind to my disquiet. But there is a domestic use of "we" as well as the royal and the editorial, and if I want a different house for the future it is in my plural capacity as family home-maker.

So a permanent base and no more upheavals. But beyond that nothing is clear. So London or country? The first fundamental. If we must choose one and give up the other, then which? Not which do we want, but which shall we give up with least regret when the time comes? For we must choose, and accept our choice, not sour a pleasant existence by considering what we are missing. Yet of all the possible sources of happiness few are valid for any one person, and it needs a surprising amount of self-knowledge to know which they will be twenty years ahead.

The present truth is clear: we want both. We want somewhere in London and somewhere in the country and a life between the two like the Emperor's Summer and Winter Palaces. That is what we have now. As well as London we have a house in the country, and if it has not been mentioned before, that is because a young woman troubled by a pea under fifty mattresses seems to me unreasonable, but to complain of discomfort through fifty more layers seems pathological. Yet I do complain. The house in the country does not suit us and we have never settled. We are no more at home than the day we moved in. The house is wrong for us and we are equally wrong for the house. We have tried for years to like it, but we never shall.

There are certain houses which seem to confirm our future.
They seem the natural setting for our particular lives, and
within their companionable shelter even sickness and sorrow
seem half-benign. But the only future I have ever imagined in
our house is showing round prospective buyers. It has always
been a house for someone else, not for us, and years of intensive
family occupation have brought us no nearer together. It is not
my doing: we none of us settle. However long we stay we shall
always be temporary occupants.

We bought it seven years ago for what seemed three good
reasons: no one else wanted it, William liked its faded Regency
graces, and I felt compelled to rescue it from the near-mortal
sickness of its long-abandoned state. It is a square and elegant
Regency villa surrounded by a garden laid out in the mid-
nineteenth century, both house and garden now plump and
flourishing after seven years nursing back to health. But what we
found at the start was a derelict house in a derelict garden. The
roof leaked disastrously; ancient trays and hip-baths, bowls and
buckets were ranged over the attic floor half-full of dirt and
rusty water. The sash-cords were broken, the stucco cracked,
the fireplaces littered with soot and birds' nests. The dark and
peeling wall-papers might have delighted a lover of Victoriana
but they did not delight us. The floors were eaten through with
damp where the cracked kitchen drain leaked under the house,
and when we pulled out the huge old dresser which covered one
side of the kitchen, the wall behind was festooned with dry-rot
like a creeper in luxuriant flower. Out of doors was as bad. The
coal shed had collapsed with the weight of wet coal-dust discarded through years, the garden-shed was a litter of mice and
rotting apples, and the garden———. But the garden I would
rather not remember even at this distance of seven years' rescue.
The garden was simply a rubbish tip.

Our love for our children, so they tell us, grows by the care
we lavish on them. Perhaps. But certainly it is not a truth which

applies to houses. For I have never lavished more care on a house than I have on the Regency Villa. Nor loved one less. It is thoroughly restored. It is dry and thriving. The roof does not leak, the floors are solid, the walls are cheerful with paper securely hung by me. But I do not love it, and it will not do. Not for us. I must resign myself to the waste of seven years' labour and accept our losses. We must change it for something else.

But for what? Is it the house that is wrong or its village setting? Is it because we are restless Londoners that we none of us stay in the country more than a day or two without leaving for somewhere else? Should we be restless like this if we gave up London for good? How can we know? How can William know who has never lived in the country as I have?

Most of us are experts at solving other people's problems, but we generally solve them in terms of our own, and the advice we give is seldom for the other people but for ourselves in their situation. Yet since one man's content is another man's misery we all need different answers to the same questions, and no one can plan another person's happiness. So I can't choose for William. But where does he *want* to live? in town or country? Certainly like every true Londoner he sighs for green fields—it is almost a test of a city-dweller that he daydream of country cottages. William loves the country as townsfolk do: because it is different from the town. But if the country were no longer a change and refreshment from something else, but his steady settled state—what then? If he crossed over, would the grass then seem greener on the other side of the fence? For William will never be a countryman. His boast will always be the townsman's boast—of how far his cottage is from the village. The countryman who lives in the cottage is only concerned with how near. On William's brief wartime visits he rejoiced in the remoteness of our farmhouse, but the children and I lived there the whole year round, and would willingly have given all the miles of green for a good red bus past the door.

Nonetheless William is firm for the country. He wants nothing better, he says, than to live with fields all round him. And what for me? The town or the country? Both now, but if I can only have one, how can I choose now for twenty years ahead?

As a child I had no doubt. In the heart of the northern industrial town where I grew up I longed and pined for the country. It was an intensity of feeling which fused my random experiences into lasting memories, and all my earliest recollections are leafy and flowery. But we change. I still want the country but I also want London, and if I had to choose only for myself I would never leave the city. Not that it is simple, even as a selfish choice. For at Christmas we were sent a horrible card of synthetic snow-glittering trees, and opening it among the mince-pies and wrapping paper, I was suddenly oblivious of the domestic bustle in a wave of longing for the fresh wet smell of woods in winter, and the cold, still, dusky air.

But not at the cost of London: the astonishing, teeming, anonymous, intelligent, swift, and various life of the city. What would it be like to live always away from the stimulus and pace of London? Doctor Johnson had no doubt about it. Those who live in the country live in jail. They are unhappy because "they have not enough to keep their minds in motion." In Johnsonian motion I suppose he means, but there are other forms of mental exercise. It is the ordinary business of living which is swifter in cities: it is skating instead of walking. And now I am used to the exhilaration of skating as the natural progression, should I get used to walking pace simply by moving house?

Or do we change again as we grow older, as we change from children to adults? And are the first and last stages our true inherent individual selves, and the busy decades of our middle life the acting out of our rôle in society as workers and social units? So that if I wanted the country as a child, shall I want it again as I grow old? Perhaps. But a great many pleasures are mutually exclusive. Few people enjoy both crowds and solitude, and our intensest pleasures are often paid for by an intense dislike of their opposite.

But not surely town and country, for here are we wanting both. The town for work perhaps, and the country for leisure. Not for week-end outings on fine summer Sundays, but to live in the country, however briefly, in all seasons and weathers: to sleep there and wake up to country mornings.

Which then for our final house? A years-old question which must now have a final answer.

But such fundamental problems are seldom decided by deliberate reasoning. They are questions we ask of our lives, not our conscious intelligence. And if we ask them early enough they answer themselves unnoticed. If we formulate and forget them the answer is there when we want it. And so it is with our house. Whatever debate and heart-searching and renunciation has gone on in my domestic unconscious, the answer is clear.

We will live in the country.

⋄⋄⋄⋄⋄ *4* ⋄⋄⋄⋄⋄

The country. As a word used by city-dwellers it is a general category, and that William and I use it as a simple alternative to London proves by itself our city status. The country—cottages of course, cows and things, in fields, woods, and hedges and so on, and life out of doors. But nothing definite. Not the Cotswolds nor the Weald of Kent, nor the Yorkshire Dales, nor the Wiltshire chalk, nor the East Anglican farmscape—countrysides as different as the different urban personalities of Birmingham or York or Brighton. The townsman's country is country as the countryman's town is town, a generic term which covers the whole area of land not already covered by cities.

Certainly William and I are Londoners, but still not so thoroughly urbanized as that. Our country is no more simply country than our town is town. We live in London, not Bristol nor Manchester nor anywhere else, and we shall consider our future country with an equal consciousness of the character of different places. We shall carefully choose.

But the places we can choose from are nonetheless limited. For we shall always want to be in touch with London. We shall never be true country people but only people who have chosen to be in the country, and that is not the same. Country people are those whose lives depend on the country; not only farmers who live by the land, but all those for whom the country is the accepted background of living, whose friends and interests are drawn from the country and whose sensibilities are adjusted to a rural setting. Country people do not go round exclaiming at the Beauties of Nature as townsfolk do; which does not mean they admire them less but that they have never known life without them. The beauties are not holiday decorations of living as savoured by city sensitives, but the unconscious natural heritage of country people.

But William and I will never qualify. However long we live away from cities we shall always now keep our urban outlook: we shall always exclaim. However deeply we bury ourselves in green our consciousness will still be nourished by cities. We shall listen to music from city orchestras, follow the news in city journals. Our friendships and interests and occupations will depend on London, not the local market town: reading books from city bookshops, writing books for city publishers. We shall always be a kind of intellectual commuter, loving the country with London sensibilities.

The moral is clear: our house in the country must be country near London; somewhere in the Home Counties—that peculiarly self-centred metropolitan label for a wide heterogeneous stretch of south-east England, as if its only valid character were its nearness to London as the self-appointed national home. It is a name which can sound contemptuous or inviting, depending on the hearer, but to us it sounds neither, it is merely a fact of location. For we have lived for years on and off in the Home Counties, and know that as the description of a surprisingly varied area it is no more helpful than town or country. To us it sounds most like a challenge, since what we want is what a great many other people want as well: a house in genuine country but within easy reach of London.

About the setting we are determined: it must be country proper, self-contained and unspoiled. No edges of beauty-spot villages, nor houses discreetly screened behind belts of trees. It must be what the boys call "owls and foxes country," looking back on their rustic childhood from the bright new lights of their city adolescence. But the owls and foxes within easy reach of London are likely to be very popular creatures, especially as our easy reach means not only easy by road but by train as well. For we know very well by long experience of country week-ending just how much we use the trains, both ourselves and for visitors. So what we want is remote country, but close to the London trains (an unlikely enough combination to begin with), and even then not simply any trains, but ones which take us to a station comfortably near to the London end of our living.

As a family we are none of us troubled by the unreasonableness of our demands, seeking perfection without apology. But even so I can't help realizing that our conditions are likely to cancel each other out. However two things are now clear: while we are still settled in London as our working base we must search for a different house in the country; we must also keep the Regency Villa in a state to tempt a buyer in exchange. And if it tempted us in its derelict condition it will surely please others in its present prosperity. It *does* please others: its Regency elegancies are much admired by all non-resident visitors.

Each week-end now I survey the house and consider it calculatingly. There must surely be people with lives it would suit even though it does not suit ours. If I repaper the attic as I always meant to, it will make an extra bedroom with its dormer window looking out over the parapet of the roof to the walnut field. I must repaint the gloomy scullery, but there is no need now to change the cream paint of the living-room to the white we like so much better. For all we know the next occupants may prefer its present butter colour, and from now on anything I do in the house will not be to please *us* but some hypothetical buyer. As for the garden, that is now merely a place to keep tidy. The grass must be mown and the hedges clipped and the borders more or less weeded, but I will plant no more trees. Short-term flowers will do well enough for the interval before we leave, and the next owners may even prefer beds of dahlias to winter-flowering evergreens.

Care-taking then for the Regency Villa. Routine, dutiful, of no more interest than housework in someone else's house. Meanwhile the search for the new house to take its place. And this time there must be no mistake, for if women start off with only so many acts of domestic creation dormant inside them like buds in a hyacinth bulb, then this is my last. I have produced three already. I can transform one more alien house to our own unmistakable family setting, but no more after that. If I move us now we must stay there.

As for the others in all this? The family quite simply don't care. They regard my domestic earthquake-making with a curious mixture of indifference, amusement, and half-pleased curiosity. "I leave it entirely to you." William makes it clear from the beginning that he takes no part in this domestic upheaval which no one but me feels the need for.

One of the many possible divisions of human beings is into those who make and those who use. Of course it is not so north-and-south simple, since human beings are too complex and changeable to be so simply divided into opposing categories, but still it is a judgment more valid and fundamental than most. There are those who produce and those who appreciate: the makers and the users. They are equally essential and equally interdependent. The makers produce the raw material for a civilized life—the houses and gardens and furniture and clothes, the books and pictures and plays and concerts—and the users combine the material selectively to a civilized way of living. Without the makers the users' life is poor and restricted: without the users the makers' talents are a sterile exercise. It is pointless to cook meals which no one enjoys, or make clothes which no one wears, or build houses whose rooms will always be empty of the life they were built for. And perhaps in the end it is more difficult to use than to make, needing wider and more varied skills, and an inborn unlearnable gift for living.

In any case we have no choice. The difference is fundamental: we are simply born one or the other in our varying degrees. And the division seems more or less equal. There are roughly as many do-it-yourself makers as appreciative users, which is fortunate for both. Certainly with William and me the categories are clear: William is user and I am maker.

But whichever may be the higher level of existence in the end, this is not the end: not the fine flowering of civilized life but only the domestic foundations of living. And in any household the housewife must necessarily be maker. She must produce what the family consumes, and that is not only meals on plates and clean shirts in drawers, but, far more important, an anchoring family base.

So William leaves it to me. Certainly he has no particular liking for the Regency Villa, but since he has never imagined anything better he accepts it on its limited merits. As a user not a maker he takes no interest in houses except to live in, and as a busy doctor he also has a strong objection to spending his leisure in domesticity. But if I see fit he will move without protest. What could be fairer?

So now for the change. First to decide the area. Near London, yes. But which side of London? However that too is already decided by William's hospitals. Unless we are to struggle across the city traffic every time we travel out, we must find a house in the area north-west of the town. So a map. With our London house as centre I draw circles of thirty- and fifty-miles radius. Thirty is the nearest in to be free of the city's ambience, fifty the most we will drive in and out at week-ends. Next I trace out the railways in the right general direction, mark with a cross the stations in my thirty- to fifty-mile belt, and draw a circle round them for the country within easy reach of the trains. Sitting in the London kitchen with the supper-table cleared and the sheets of the one-inch Ordnance map spread out before me, I am delighted by my orderly efficiency.

And as a method my circles have the merit of immediately reducing the search to a manageable area. But reducing it most alarmingly I suddenly realize. For there are less than a dozen stations both near enough in and far enough out, and if I draw an outline on the map to take them in, the stretch of country it encloses is mostly the Chiltern Hills.

Very well. We will live in the Chilterns. A logical, suitable, and altogether satisfactory decision. For the hills and the Vale of Aylesbury below them are country we already know well from years of living. Our farmhouse was in the Vale—it still is in its now disenchanted state. The Regency Villa is in a village at the foot of the scarp, at "the rootes of the hills" as Leland calls it. This has been our adopted country for so long now that we feel it our own. We know it not by cold information but by feeling. Our lives have happened here. In this contrasted landscape of hills and plain we have been happy and sad, lonely and despondent, or peacefully content. The children have grown up with one foot in London and one in this country, equally at home in either.

Here then we belong, as far as Londoners belong anywhere

in the country, and here we will settle, either in the Chiltern Hills, or where the long rolling plateau of the upland country drops at a sudden swift scarp to the dim blue distances of the Vale of Aylesbury.

❖❖❖❖❖ 5 ❖❖❖❖❖

A house in the country. We have chosen which country. Now to find the house. We consider houses. Consider and marvel and look away. What we realize we must learn to do early on is translate house-agents' descriptions into reality, and before they start off, all prospective house-buyers should compile their own house-hunting dictionary of phrase and fable.

Excellent possibilities for conversion—the house is a near-ruin.

A productive garden—a cabbage-patch instead of lawn.

Mature—neglected.

Near shops and station—trains thunder past the windows.

London thirty minutes—a single express-train a day. By local train one hour. By road an hour and a half if lucky.

Three quarters of all praise must be discounted, and any desirable features, from water-supply to garden, unless specifically mentioned are almost certainly lacking.

We decipher the descriptions and inspect the realities, but to describe the many desirable residences we have looked at is only to recall past sorrow and profitlessly to deepen disillusion. They will not do (to understate the undesirable is perhaps the best use of understatement). Very well. The agents have nothing to offer. Nothing even remotely as attractive as the Regency Villa we plan to leave. But perhaps it is only that the houses we would like are not for sale, but are cherished by their satisfied owners. Suppose we ignore the owners. Are there any houses we would like if we could have them? For we are in no real hurry despite my impatience. We can stay where we are and wait.

A house in the country—for us it is not a vague category but an exact description. We don't want a cottage in a village, nor a house on the edge of a town, nor a gentleman's residence in a park. We want a plain house and we want it in open country. And houses in country are hard to come by. We consider everything we see, ignoring the fact that its owners are solidly settled inside it. Suppose it were empty (we have disposed of dozens of unsuspecting householders): would we like it? But even so, we find nothing exactly right. In the kind of place we want, there are seldom any houses to consider—it is the chief reason why the places please us, such is our perversity. Or if we do discover the right situation with a building already there, then it is either a farm-labourer's cottage or a farmer's farm, some true working part of the countryside and not something to be used merely as a home for city migrants.

It is not encouraging. But neither is it as depressing as it ought to be. For instead of a gloomy acceptance of facts and a reconciled making-do with the Regency Villa, I am dazzled by a glorious new idea rising over the horizon like the morning sun. We want a house. We can't find one we like. Why not build one ourselves?

Why *not?* If other people build houses, why not us? We know what we want: we have a house we can sell to pay for it; I have an architect brother to design it. So why not? It is not what we first intended, but it very soon becomes what I long to do above all else. For the idea of building one's own domestic snail-shell is irresistible. We most of us live in a succession of houses, each only more or less right for our particular domestic life, and by adapting them as best we can we learn exactly what we want as a container for our own way of living. We learn too that we never find it in a house built for someone else's domesticity: that the only exactly right shell for any snail is the one it secretes itself.

We could build a house. It is a dazzling new idea which transforms my end-of-winter malaise to irrepressible delight. And if I must be maker instead of user, what better to make than a house?

But even so entrancing a prospect does not quite blind me to the truth I have gradually learnt from living with myself all these years—that where houses are concerned I am unreliable always. Not unreliable about the houses, but about myself. My enthusiasm outrides all caution and common sense. Certainly, since I am a willing and hard-working horse, I should be given my head when once on the road, but someone else should decide on the road. William must say. For William is not carried away, as I am, by the very idea of a house. He has saved us already, thank goodness, from a seven-bedroom farm on the Pembroke-shire coast and a miniature palace in Provence on sale for a song. So William must decide.

"Shall we sell the Regency Villa and build a new house?"

"Yes." He is prompt and definite. "If that's what you want and you think you can do it. Yes. It's an excellent idea. Why don't you start straight away?" When William decides on the road, he also believes in galloping.

And so I will start. The prospect stretches gloriously ahead. But what I have no idea of at this visionary beginning is the enormous amount of grindingly hard work I shall have to put into the undertaking. For nearly three years the whole of my life will be house. Our comfortable domestic rhythm will be disrupted, my private life forgotten, and I shall be conscious of nothing at all but the house in creation. It will absorb every hour of leisure, every flicker of energy. I shall cease to be a normal human being and become a mere catalyst for converting ideas and materials and labour into a building with a garden round it. And all for pleasure! For a fanciful whim of liking one walled enclosure for living better than another. I am producing my own domestic earthquake and I shall find that the effort is utterly exhausting.

But in the beginning I have no suspicion of the rigours ahead. The beginning is as treacherously easy as the smooth stretch of river before a waterfall. I begin to look for a site to build on, and looking for a site without bothering about building permission is like shopping without bothering about the bill. It is wonderfully easy, a gloriously irresponsible self-indulgence. It is a creative pleasure with none of the labour of creation, and my week-ends now are a secret delight which I look forward to all the London week. On Friday evenings I study the map and mark out an area to search for a site. On Saturday mornings we go out to the country, and after lunch I set off to explore my chosen stretch of the Chiltern Hills. Wouldn't anyone like to come with me? Won't William come? But no. They are not interested. A plot of ground for an imaginary house for a new way of imaginary living. How can they be expected to concern themselves with anything so unrealistic? Nor will I persuade such earth-bound companions. I leave them and set off.

There are all kinds of ways of exploring the countryside but none as entirely satisfactory as this. I drive slowly about the lanes and look at the landscape, and when I discover some particularly beautiful stretch, I find the best view-point, imagine our house there, and sit and admire the prospect. It is a particular form of daydreaming which Thoreau describes exactly.

"At a certain season of our life we are accustomed to consider every spot as the possible site of a house. . . . Wherever I sat, there I might live, and the landscape radiated from me accordingly; there I might live, I said, and there I did live, for an hour a summer and a winter life."

That is it exactly. But does it then happen to everyone—this urge to build a house as a bird builds a nest? Is it nothing to do with feminine instincts, as I always thought, but simply a symptom of our middle-age, as nest-building is a sign of spring? For

Moving. *Why?*

Thoreau is an uncommitted bachelor, and certainly he knows all about it. "At a certain season of our life," he says, as if it were a common observation. "We are accustomed," he says, as if it were the most ordinary thing in the world to find reasonable people sitting about in fields, engrossed in a sudden consciousness of the landscape radiating from their centre like the rays of a sun. Perhaps he is right and this building of imaginary houses belongs to a particular season of all our lives, like love-affairs or wanting to be farmers. Certainly this year it has come upon me as irresistibly as in our youth the urge to independence drives us away from home. I have sat and lived about the countryside as Thoreau did, scrambled through dozens of hedges (there was no bother with hedges, one supposes, in the woods of New England) to consider a phantom dwelling in the field beyond. I have explored dozens of lanes and side-roads, hoping to find some particular corner where a house would fit as exactly as a cup on a saucer. Time after time I have chosen just the right hollow or hill-side, some level space facing south and sheltered from the wind, and time after time have reduced the countryside to a prospect from our various imaginary windows, changing the living-room from south to west, moving the house a few yards up-hill or down to compose the view more perfectly in the window-frame. The landscape of the Chiltern Hills has radiated from me from a hundred different focal points, and I too have lived for days, weeks, whole summer seasons, in a score of different houses in these brief winter week-ends. When the urge is strong upon me I have only to pause at the corner of a field or the edge of a wood and I am at once enclosed by a shadowy house. The walls rise round me, the roof is suspended above my head, the windows not only frame the view exactly in space, but already the curtains are up, they sway and billow in the summer breeze, are drawn across the calm frosty nights of winter. I have opened the door to the dewy morning day after day, watched the slanting light across the evening fields a hundred times, lived long contented summer days between the sunny phantom kitchen and the flowery image of a garden. In my house-building moods I secrete houses as naturally as a hen lays eggs. It is scarcely even a conscious process, I *exude* imaginary houses whether I will or not.

But none of them, alas, are houses which will shelter us from real-life weather. We shall never get anything built by my sitting about in the corners of fields and feeling myself a soul-mate of Thoreau. So I realize brutally clearly as soon as I begin to ask about building. For if we want a house in a field we are as likely to be let put it in the middle of Hyde Park as most of the sites I have built on. The Chiltern Hills are unspoilt country. On their rounded slopes we could find a hundred places for our house. But why they are still unspoilt is precisely because no one is let build the hundred houses to spoil them. Is not let build even a single house—so I soon begin despairingly to feel. For my inquiries discover nothing but refusals. No building there—nothing beyond that boundary—nothing on that side of the top road—nothing but farm-workers' cottages—nothing at all in any of that area.

Beautiful. Unspoilt. Near to London. To balance such weighty positives there must clearly be a great many negatives too. But still it seems astonishing that so large a number of public bodies can be needed to protect so small a stretch of country. For the County Council and Rural District Council are only the beginning of a list which goes on through National Trust, Forestry Commission, Green Belt, private estates, special areas, and the like—a band of virtuous interests united to keep the country as country, and not let Londoners like us turn it into an outer suburb. In the first sharp discouragement, I feel that a jig-saw map of their various spheres of influence would cover every inch of the countryside. Cover it many times over, for variously protected areas overlap each other, and some of the lovelier stretches are guarded by half-a-dozen fiercely active defenders.

Wherever I turn now, the most prominent feature I am conscious of is a NO TRESPASSING notice, generally invisible but still overwhelmingly real. The most ordinary green fields—so I find now I try to invade them—are surrounded by impregnable ramparts of restrictions to keep out people exactly like us.

The more perfect the place for a house, the more perfectly unattainable. It is like falling in love with one's enemy—not even with an enemy, since the bonds of mutual hate are as strong as love, but with someone who coldly denies our living existence. The week-end search, which began like a visit to a Christmas toyshop, is now like the treatment of alcoholics. The certainty of being denied is the drug which destroys all pleasure in what I long for. The very beauty of the Chiltern country is now the most penetrating poison, for I swallow it whole and it turns sour inside me. I come unexpectedly on some new valley or view of the hills never noticed before, and stop in sudden delight. But as if a light were put out as I entered a room, my first delight changes to a guilty sense of rejection. I am not wanted here. I am undesirable. Unseen enemies resist my presence and drive me emotionally away. The very landscape seems to deny me, and the fields and woods to hold aloof from my unwanted admiration. The more warmly I love the more coldly I am rejected.

No doubt everyone suffers his own particular version of angst and this is mine—the guilty misery of not being wanted. There are dark week-ends when my enthusiasm shrinks like a hot-house plant put out in the killing weather, and the east winds of my winter are the planners and their many allies. They are now my foes. I hate the whole army of restrictive bodies who keep us away. I no longer feel they are guarding the countryside for all to enjoy, us included; instead they are keeping us out for some secret and selfish purpose of their own. They have become the unknown enemy, my particular category of the universal malevolence which besets us, entrenched and powerful and obscure. The innocent well-meaning planners have become my "They."

PART TWO

SEARCHING.

WHERE?

6

AT WEEK-ENDS I LOVE THE COUNTRY AND hate Them. In the London week between, I reason myself into reconciliation. For of course one wants the restrictions, wants one's chosen countryside kept safe from invasion by vandals like us. It is only that we all want some loop-hole to slip through ourselves. *We* must edge in quickly through the closing door, but after that—no one. The park gates must be shut and locked behind us and the rest of the world kept safely outside.

Of course we are atrociously selfish. But I have noticed that everyone feels the same, even though they may not admit it, or if they do admit, then are cheerfully unashamed. "We were lucky to build when we did," they tell us. "This is all protected now." Or, "It spoils our view," they complain—*our* view—as if we owned the entire landscape simply because we have built a house to face in a certain direction. Or if they feel safe from intrusion, they boast shamelessly of their good fortune: "We shall never be spoilt here you know. It's National Trust for as far as you can see."

As for us, we ask nothing better than to join the boasters; for the Chiltern Hills, as we now well know, are exactly the place one boasts of. To build a house in their lovelier stretches is very much a matter of slipping last in through the rapidly closing door. So it is no use choosing a field and expecting to build: that is like trying to get through the locked door simply by pushing. We must start the other way round: find out what is allowed, and search the countryside in terms of it.

For certainly *something* is allowed, or there would not be odd houses going up in ones and twos in so many places. Not that they are ever in the kind of places we are looking for, but still some building is certainly considered, even by planners as anxious as we soon shall be ourselves, so we hope, to prevent any further building-spread in a sweep of country so perilously exposed to London. We thoroughly approve in principle, it is only that we want to cross the barrier and see the defences working from the other side. We want to be the defended, not the invaders. And I suppose everyone, if they were honest enough to admit it, would like all rules to apply to other people but not to themselves. We want the planners to prevent others annoying us, but to leave us free to annoy other people. Yet since the proportion of others to us is likely to be at least a hundred to one, the planners are on our side by even the most selfish calculation. And to the conscientious (which I am in my better moments) the planning authorities bring a different kind of benefit. For the planning officials are our social conscience supplied to us free by the Welfare State. Whether we like it or not they prevent us from doing what we ought not to do as members of society. Naturally we don't like it, especially since planners are not supplied on demand like National Health doctors, but forced on us willy-nilly like policemen.

But even so they are easier to deal with than a personally supplied conscience, which rouses all manner of contradictory and inhibiting emotions. With the planners as mentors we are irresponsibly free again of the complications of the adult state: we are quite simply determined to get our own way. No need for disinterested judgments: that is their business, not ours. We have delegated our uncomfortable conscience, and if it agrees, then all is socially well.

The situation is simple then. We want to build a house in the Chiltern Hills; the Chilterns are protected by planners; we must find a site they agree to. But before we can come to terms with an opponent we must first get to know him; so the next move is clear: I must go and see the planners and ask them the rules of the game.

Planners are on the side of the angels.

I would like to be on the side of the angels, but my virtue is unreliable in matters that concern me as closely as building a house.

It is important to state the large facts in calm detachment before the contest begins. For I am not naturally either patient or reasonable, and like most housewives, I have lived a great many years now with only the restrictions I see fit to accept. My natural reaction to planners is to disagree with their judgment and fulminate against their rules, which trip up my racing enthusiasm. But I do not quarrel with their fundamental faith: that the countryside is far more important than anyone's house. Of course it is in this overcrowded island. It is only that when the house is our own our values are violently distorted. The house looms so very large to our near view, the injury to the country beyond looks so very slight.

But planners, so I reassure myself, have an in-built sense of proportion, and all the powers they need to impose it on selfish private citizens. I will go and see them. I write for an appointment. We exchange dates. I am prompt on the doorstep. It is a morning in early spring with the sun dazzling in the window and a sense of summer exhilaratingly round the corner. He offers me a chair. He is discreetly welcoming. What can he do for me?

"We want to build a house."

"Yes," he says, and waits.

"We want it in the country. We would like to build it somewhere in the Chiltern Hills."

"I see," he says. He is utterly non-committal. Whatever his inner reaction, there is no way of guessing it from his outward behaviour.

"Why have you come to see me?"

This is a move as direct as my house-building statement, but I am not skilled as he is at avoiding direct answers.

"Well," I say. "We know about needing planning permission. It would be a great help if you would tell us what conditions it is given on."

"There are a great many difficulties," he says (he is certainly an expert at parrying, but on the whole not unfriendly); and he gives me a private lecture on the many difficulties, about which I in my turn am equally non-committal.

"Yes," I say. "We realize the difficulties. But will you tell us what is allowed?"

However he is not yet prepared to answer so direct a question. He leans back in his chair and looks at me under his spectacles. Do we realize that he only represents the local Council? And even if they were prepared to consider a house, there are a great many other bodies to satisfy too. And he repeats with understandable relish the long list of public guardians I know already, even adding a few more abstruse-sounding titles I have never heard of.

"Yes," I say. "We know about the bodies. We know it isn't easy. But will you tell us what the Council would allow as a start?"

I have no doubt he is used to dealing with people like me—Londoners whose immediate reaction to an unspoilt stretch of country is to rush in and build on it, as children rush to trample over untrodden snow.

"Why do you want to live in this particular part of the country?" He has evaded my question again to examine us (or so I hope) as possible inhabitants of his domain. I consider him carefully: my professional Welfare-State-style social conscience made incarnate and sitting in judgment in the opposite chair.

A public office at half-past ten in the morning is no place to discuss the growing of roots, though I think he would sympathize, for most of the country planners I have met are as thoroughly rooted as farmers in the area they belong to. But I put it obliquely and hope he will understand.

"We have half-lived out here for a long time," I tell him. "Our children grew up on a farm in the Vale."

"Whereabouts?" He asks, suddenly interested. I tell him.

"Isn't there an old Tudor house there that's scheduled as an Ancient Monument?"

"Yes. That's the one we lived in. We were very fond of the old farmer."

"Oh, yes. We knew him too. Only too well. The Council had endless trouble with him right through the war. Very independent he was. He simply ignored all regulations. He seemed to consider the planners were only there to annoy him."

He looks at me quizzically.

"Well, here I am," I protest, "taking all sorts of notice of the regulations."

"So I see," he says, but his smile is ambiguous.

We have a house in the village now, I tell him, and I describe which one.

Yes, he says. He knows it. He drives past it every day and often wondered whose it was. He greatly admires the garden, he adds. Especially the old trees along the hedge. It's the pleasantest stretch of the road from the village.

This seems hopeful and I wait for him to go on.

Well, he says at last. Their general policy is—and I am given a short lecture on the difficulties of preserving country so dangerously near London etc. etc. It is a lecture I am by now almost as well-qualified as he is to repeat to the thoughtless.

Yes, I agree, and wait for him to go on. But it is my move it seems, in this wary walking around each other—he saying nothing to commit himself and me saying nothing to disqualify us.

Yes, I agree again. But we've noticed houses being built, and some of them are in country places. Will he tell us what conditions they are allowed on?

Well, he says, leaning back expansively in his chair and answering me at last. They have a policy of in-filling and rounding-off. (He produces these specialized conceptions of planners as if they must be perfectly self-evident to everyone.)

If the house is suitable, he says, and harmonizes with its surroundings, then they allow in-filling and rounding-off. At least (and here he takes fright at such an open invitation to build) a certain amount, and in certain places. It all depends (he is retreating fast to his former reserve).

But never mind, I have found what we want. If a village has spread in irregular bulges, we can round off the boundary and build a house in the bay between the bulges. Or anyway *hope* to build one. Or better still, we can in-fill: we can look for a straggle of cottages in open country and fill in a space between them. It is like being told officially exactly what is allowed through the Customs (which we never are).

The interview is over. I thank him. We shake hands. We are still friends. In this first stage of the manœuvres I have made solid progress, for I realize by his wariness that of all the authorities we must come to terms with before we are accepted, he is probably the most important.

Round-off and in-fill, in-fill and round-off. Wonderful words. They run in my head in rhymes like Miss Buss and Miss Beale. They are purest poetry. For if poetry depends on the emotive power of the words it uses, the power of these is emotive enough to give life to whole volumes of mediocre verse. No universal words from the dark beginnings of language now hold for me the evocative wealth of these awkward syllables. All edges of all villages are contained in the sonorous circles of rounding-off. In-fill with its narrow parallels is the very pattern of country lanes thinly scattered with cottages. And they are positive conceptions, weapons to keep off the invisible enemies who meet me wherever I turn. I can explore the country now on terms more or less my own. And though it will be a restricted view through the narrowish blinkers of in-filling and rounding-off, at least it will not be automatically closed to all comers.

"They" are no longer sinister. It is not exactly that we have joined them, and certainly they are not on our side. But they are neutral. They are judges now, more or less fair. They are the British Police again and not the Gestapo.

As for finding a site—so far my search has been as unrealistic as Icarus' flight. I have tried to fly by visions instead of by the inescapable facts of how heavy bodies are supported in air. Now my fine wings have melted; but still I have not drowned like poor improvident Icarus, but fallen on dry land however stony. I can get up and start again more modestly. From now on the journey will be laboriously on foot, but if I walk hard and patiently enough we may still arrive.

❖❖❖❖❖ 7 ❖❖❖❖❖

Enthusiasm is a plant which grows variously in the varying soils of different natures. In reasonable people it conforms to reasonable restrictions, as the eighteenth century knew, but to the impatient, opposition is a stimulus which they take off against like aeroplanes into the wind. I know I am more impatient than reasonable, but to be fair it is not so much the opposition to our building which now spurs me on, as the fear that the door is irrevocably closing, that unless we slip through quickly and find our site soon, then we never shall. Certainly the very real difficulties of doing anything have stiffened to determination our first vague idea of doing something, sometime, not too far off. We must do it *now*. Perhaps not build the actual house straight away, but at least make sure of a site with permission to build when we sell the Regency Villa. I must start the search again; but realistically this time—no dreaming or Beauties of Nature: no nonsense of any kind. I must put on my sensible shoes, if I can find them, and go steadily plodding.

So. I plod. I am reasonable. I calculate.

First. The situation. Anything we achieve will have to be a compromise between us and the planners.

Second. The facts. What we want—unrestricted Thoreau-style choice. What the planners want—nothing.

Third. The compromise. The planners will allow in-filling and rounding-off. We will be satisfied with—but what? That we must formulate exactly before we begin.

Unspoilt

Country

In the Chiltern Hills,

Farmland from choice.

Within walking distance of one of three stations.

(Only three now—the rest are variously unsatisfactory.)

With a view,

Facing South.

A largish garden.

Water, electricity, and telephone near at hand.

But is this really compromise I wonder? I doubt whether the planners would think so. It would certainly satisfy us, but then it would be hard to see how it could fail to. Never mind, we will bring down our standards if we must, but at least we will set off with them high, like aiming above a target to allow for the fall on the way.

Searching. *Where?*

Further facts. If we are ever to find our site I must go out and hunt for it. Nothing is likely to be offered by obliging land-agents to people who sit hopefully about and wait for plums to be popped into their mouths.

So I will go out and hunt. But this time no wandering down inviting lanes or enthusing over views. First the local land-agents. It is not that I imagine their books are full of desirable plots waiting for us to put a house on. If their books are full at all it will be with lists of people waiting for building-sites like hungry sea lions waiting to grab at fish in the zoo. I shall visit the agents for information, as a way of surveying our chosen country.

I make a list of all the house-agents in the area and call on them all. There are a great many. I say my piece: that we want a site to build a house on in unspoilt country etc. etc. I produce my demand as nonchalantly as a child asking for the moon as a birthday present, and it amuses me to watch their reaction. It is always the same: a perfectly genuine horror at the enormity of what I am suggesting. Fools rush in (so they politely imply). I have no idea what I am asking (but indeed I have). No building is allowed anywhere in the area without special permission. Permission is impossible to get. The kind of site we want would never come on to the market in any case—and so on and so on. They will let us know if anything etc. etc. But really they can't help me. Good morning.

I long ago noticed that this is always the first reaction if we ask people for anything difficult. It is partly I think to make us realize the outrageousness of our request, and partly an unconscious ceremony to enhance the value of what they might just possibly produce in the end. It is, in any case, a natural defence against our generally quite unreasonable demands.

The agent who found us our house in London has long been our friend. And one day he told me that even if he knew he had the exactly right house for a customer, he never produced it at once. If he did they would be sure to find fault with it. He had learnt by years of experience to show them other unsuitable houses first, and only to bring out the right one when they had seen enough wrong ones to appreciate its merits. How many wrong ones had he sent us to see? I asked him. Only two he said, we were ready by the third.

So I say my piece, the agents say theirs, and none of them show me anything either right or wrong.

But as a plodder I have a great deal more stamina than as a field-corner dreamer. No angst this time. No misery of rejection. I accept their denials without dismay and interpret them to suit the situation:—that what we want is hard to come by (this is not news). They are not going to the trouble of finding it for us (and why should they?). If we want our site I must go out and produce it myself.

And so I will. For I know this particular country far better than they do sitting at their office desks, and besides I have a secret weapon in my In-filling and Rounding-off, a pair of binoculars to spy out plots of land the agents know nothing about.

No one is offering sites for sale, not at two a penny nor at any other more likely price. So much is certainly clear as soon as I start. There is nothing for sale. But that does not necessarily mean there is nothing to buy. For any change of ownership involves two different people, the seller and the buyer, and the initiative for the exchange may come from either. In a town it is generally the seller who announces his goods for sale, and the buyers who come if they are interested. But in the country it is as likely as not the buyer who makes the first move. I have lived in the country for ten years, and I know the old-fashioned countryman's dislike of going out with his goods into the public market and exposing himself to all comers. If Farmer Adams has a cow too many he does not put up a notice of sale with a price on. He waits for Farmer Goodman to come along and ask him what about that odd heifer of his that he hasn't rightly much use for? Had he thought of getting rid of it? And what sort of price had he thought of?

Not that the inquiry goes on at anything like so breakneck a speed. There are soundings and probings, long pauses and slow considerations. A full-stop between sentences is a whole circuit of the cowsheds and barns, and half-an-hour leaning on the pig-sty wall. But odd plots of land in the country are much like cows: they are surplus bits of the farm that the farmer hasn't rightly much use for, but never gets round to doing anything about. If anyone is interested they'll make him an offer and then he'll consider.

In any case the smart house-agents of the Home Counties are exactly the kind of person that old-fashioned farmers most dis-trust. "Agent" to them is a sinister word like "dealer" at auction sales. During the war, when William was posted to an Air Force camp in an area near London where even pig-sties were treas-ured as palaces because of the German bombing, we found our Tudor farmhouse standing empty in its orchard and we rented it from the farmer for thirty shillings a week with no more ado and to our long-lasting mutual satisfaction.

Why hadn't he put it in an agent's hands instead of leaving it empty? So I asked him once as he sat and drank tea in our farmhouse kitchen and played with the children.

"Oh. I've never fancied doing business through agents and such like. You never know where you are with 'em. Never can trust 'em. The old house was well enough empty for a bit. Come to no harm and I weren't in no hurry. Thought I'd just wait and see who came after it, and if I liked the look of 'em, then they could have it."

Our farmer was a treasure among countrymen, but in no way unique. And since change is slow in the country I trust that farmers may still not fancy the new-style agents, but will be waiting till I come along to ask about that odd bit of land be-tween the hayricks and the edge of the road—awkward to plough and no good for grazing. Why not sell it to us to build a house on instead of leaving it to grow nettles? (Though naturally I would not mention the nettles, but only imply them.)

The farmer would look at me suspiciously and say: Well, he'd never considered selling any land—he'd never thought about it—he didn't know—and such like humming and hawing while he examined such a novel idea and wondered whether he'd like me for a neighbour.

And I would make conversation while he got used to this unexpected invasion of his settled state. I would tell him how we used to live on a farm in the Vale, and did he know farmers X and Y? (Proving, I hoped, that we were country-folk ourselves and no strange city species.) Then I would wait, and after a pause he would say: Well, he didn't know. He'd never liked the idea of selling away land. True that bit I mentioned weren't much use to him. But still he didn't know. How much did we reckon it was worth?

Not that he would really ask such a point-blank question, especially at so early a stage of the proceedings. But to the question when it did eventually come, I would know the proper and expected answer: That we couldn't be both buyer and seller, and that he must name his own price.

However this is scarcely any more constructive as progress than building imaginary houses: it is only a different variety of daydreaming. For we have found no plot—between wood-edge and hayricks or anywhere else. I have not even started to search. But now I will. I organize. For if family week-ends in the country are to leave the housewife time for her own concerns, they must be organized to an efficient routine. It begins on Friday. I work out the week-end meals—shop and cook—make cakes—fill casseroles with meals which only need warming. Making sure that even my more-or-less helpless all-male family can feed themselves without me if need be.

On Saturday morning we pack the car (I fume at their lei-

surely all-the-time-in-the-world pace) and down to the country
in time for lunch. Then with plates washed up almost before
they are empty, Saturday afternoon is free. I shall be back for
supper, I tell them, but if anyone wants tea (so I tell myself)
they must help themselves. I shall not be there.

Lie-abed Sunday mornings are more difficult to organize
until I harden my heart and leave them to get their own break-
fasts. Then I am up and off in the sunshiny spring weather,
only begrudging the Sunday lunch which brings me back to my
housewifely duties.

Saturday afternoons and Sunday mornings. The Search.
Would anyone like to come with me? It seems to me incredible
that any of them could want to do anything else. But they in-
credibly do, and I soon learn better than to invite them. And the
Search? It is very methodical. I work out on the map an area for
each week-end. Within the area I circle each possible village,
looking for spaces left haphazard between buildings, and drive
down every likely looking lane of straggling cottages.

Rounding-off and in-filling. They really are words to con-
jure with; for despite all the house-agents' denials there are
building-sites to be found, now I search for them thoroughly
enough. There are even sites already for sale if we want them—
not with placards put up and notices sent out, and admittedly not
for sale through the agents, but nonetheless, when I find the
owners and ask, already for sale and the price more or less decided.

However even what I think of as our compromise standards
prove to be extremely exacting, and the sites I find are so far
from reaching them that there is nothing yet worth considering
seriously. And even the perfect site would be suspect, for
though it might be perfect now, what is there to stop other
people like us rounding-off all round us? We are unashamedly
selfish.

8

March has gone and half of April. A gentle spring and the hills never lovelier. The warblers are back in the new green hedges and in mid-April I find our site. It is waiting for me in the sun one Sunday morning, a level stretch half-way up the slope of the Chiltern scarp and looking out over the wide rolling sea of the Vale of Aylesbury, which stretches mistily blue with increasing distance to the dim horizon.

Yes. It is for sale.

Yes. We should get planning permission.

Yes. The price is reasonable even by our somewhat innocent standards.

I stand in the middle of the acre or so of flowery grass, and half-expect to soar with excitement into the empty blue sky like the larks above me.

But I batten down my exhilaration and try not to build a house round myself straight away, but to concentrate on a cold-blooded assessment of good and bad qualities.

The setting? Perfect. A wide flat terrace with a lane along the edge: the Vale in front, a wooded hill-side behind, and above that a long stretch of hills guaranteed safe by the National Trust.

London? Less than forty miles away.

The station? A mile down the road.

Neighbours for in-filling? Out of sight round a bend in the lane.

Electricity and telephone? The wires are at the road-side. And certainly water, for there is an F.H. post at the gate to the field, and though I have never known what F.H. stands for I know it means water.

Searching. *Where?*

So will this do at last? What more could we possibly hope for? Very cautiously I let the house grow round me. With the living-room looking out over the Vale, and the clutter of the house (entrance and stairs and pantry and bathroom) facing back to the hill-side. I imagine our life here—William going off walking over the hills, the boys cycling down to the village, friends coming out from London, me gardening. Yes. It all fits. Especially the gardening. For this is a perfect place for a garden, sheltered from wind, and set about with the flowery shrubs of the chalk-hills. And it has trees already—eight, nine—no, ten well-grown beeches, which will be *ours* if we buy the land.

It is one of my lasting astonishments that trees are held of such little account that they simply go with the ground they stand on and no more ado. Yet trees are such treasure, such positive gain. Here are ten beeches, growing for at least as long as I have lived, the true owners of the soil, magnificent creatures inhabiting this acre of hill-side like reigning princes. And if we buy the land they will belong to us. We shall *own* ten beech-trees. Perhaps if we place the house carefully we can frame the view between their smooth trunks as if between pillars. But not too close because of shading the windows. Which way is south?

And suddenly my house collapses in ruins about me. For this will not do. The south is in the wrong direction. The scarp of the Chilterns faces north-west across the plain below, and if we build our house here, then rooms with a view will be rooms without sun.

In building a house, there are a great many disadvantages which can be overcome by careful designing, but, alas, the angle of the sun is not one of them. Short of Old-Testament-style miracles it is one of the unalterable facts which we have to accept without argument. The mid-day sun shines from the south. We want the sun. A house facing north will be sunless. We will not build here. I may feel sick with disappointment, but the logic is brutally final.

The sun is one of the reasons we are leaving our Regency Villa, a house which cares so little for sun in the windows that the whole south front is shaded by a veranda. "Oh! A Trafalgar roof! How delightful!" So knowledgeable visitors exclaim with enthusiasm, admiring the shallow pagoda curve and the wrought iron railing and the cut-out edging like a wooden awning. But then they are visitors, they never have to live in the rooms so constantly shaded by their Trafalgar roof. And we do. We never again want a house where we look out from gloomy rooms to a garden brilliant with sunshine. There is never too much sun in England, and if there is, then we will have Venetian blinds at the south windows and make patterns of stripes on the ceiling by moving the slats. It is what I have always wanted, and I much prefer movable slats to immovable Trafalgar roofs.

So this will not do. I must go on searching. It is like failing an examination and realizing I must start all over again.

Giving up the beech-trees is a dreadful wrench. And the view—while I sit and lament the intransigent sun, the melting distance has deepened to the blue of the sea at evening. Oh dear. Today I can search no further. I shall go home and have tea with the family and grieve for my ten lost beech-trees.

Mid-April. The end of April. The beginning of May. I plod as I promised and try to dissociate feeling from logic. On Saturday afternoons I look for sites; on Sunday mornings I take the family to see them. But since they do no searching, and since they are in any case quite content in the shady Regency Villa, they are most exactingly critical of everything I find. Nothing will do—too close, too far, no view, no sun, too steep, too flat—they have dozens of valid objections besides the ones I often believe they make up to annoy me.

As the spring progresses the edge of the Chilterns is littered with sites discovered and rejected. What I could do, I suppose, is set up as house-agent myself and sell off the sites to people more tolerant than we are.

Searching. *Where?*

Mid-May and the hill-sides are scribbled over with miles of blossoming hawthorn hedges. If I had eyes for anything else but in-filling and rounding-off it would be a weekly pleasure to drive about the flowery lanes and look at the countryside. But the stirring spring only stirs my impatience to a more painful intensity. My season blossoms with disappointments instead of flowers.

Then one bright Saturday afternoon another site. Edging off a road we have driven down dozens of times is a tiny lane we never noticed, for since it leads to nowhere but a gate on the edge of a wood, there is no sign-post to mark its secretive slipping away from the road behind a clump of trees, a narrow winding lane wandering towards the hills, with on one side a curving shoulder of cornfield against the sky, and on the other a straggle of houses. Houses with a gap between them, about half-an-acre of field on the side of one of the shallow inlying valleys of the chalk, and looking along the main gap through the hills.

The gate to this possible Eden stands invitingly open, a field-gate sunk on its hinges through years of neglect and permanently tethered now by ropes of brambles. As I go in from the lane two yellow-hammers fly up from their foraging in the dry tangle of last year's uncut grass.

Will it do—this brambly birdy flowery patch of field?

This time the sun and the view coincide: it is the first thing I check. A view of fields and woods and the rounded hills flowing into each other in the distance, and lit now reassuringly from the right by the westering sun. The station is closer than before, only a footpath away over the cornfield, and the straggle of houses are clearly houses with water and electricity.

Will it do? I have learnt to be cautious, to control my rising exhilaration and save myself from the despairing distance it plunges again with disappointment. But will it do?

I admire the view, but restrainedly. I consider the sun with as much satisfaction as if I myself had arranged its direction across the sky. I grow confident. Surely. Yes. I fight down jubilation and look for objections. But *what* objections? There are none that I can see. Admittedly no beech-trees are included this time, but there are plenty of well-grown shrubs—dogwoods and buckthorns and sloes and hawthorns and way-faring trees and travellers' joy in a thick-growing tangle. Apart from the un-known price and the planning permission (we should clearly be in-filling), surely it will do.

"You're pleased about something." Even the family notice at supper. "You'd better tell us what you've found." So all off together to inspect on Sunday morning, and this time even the critical family committee can find no objections. Not that the boys stay to look for them. They survey. They approve. Then they rattle off down the lane on their shaky bicycles back to their usual Sunday morning with friends in the village. Only William stays to consider together. We sit where the house will be and look out through the living-room window. The patch of field may only be half an acre but the view is uninterrupted miles. The sun is a reassuring dazzle direct in our mid-day eyes.

Yes. This time surely yes. We are both agreed. This is seri-ous enough for me to stay down till Monday and find out who it belongs to and whether they will sell it. Surely the three of them can look after themselves in London for a single night (it is William's surely, not mine) and I can get back in time for Mon-day supper. (Even the perfect site, I notice, must not interfere with more than one evening meal.)

The car is packed. They are off. I am left alone with my satisfaction, and I spend the evening in that most entrancing of all pastimes—designing houses on scraps of paper. For although the main outlines have always been clear, the arrangement of rooms varies with the setting. The living-room here perhaps. No. *Here.* The kitchen there and the door here—no, *here*— (more scribbling-out and rearranging of rectangles)—and the bedrooms all facing south. Bother. Forgotten the staircase. But there are never any stairs in beginners' houses: it is a well-known architectural fact. And anyway I must go to bed (goodness! it's after midnight) and be businesslike tomorrow.

The site will do. We can have it. They are facts which illuminate the London week, and by the following week-end we feel ourselves already so firmly installed that William and I go walking in the fields and woods which from now on will be our own particular corner of the country—miles of country with not so much as a single house in the whole morning's wandering.

Looking back I am astonished that we ever imagined we should find a place to suit us. We started by making out a list of conditions which are in no way a compromise but a straightforward demand for perfection. "All of which," as Bacon says in his *Essay on Building*, "as it is impossible perhaps to find together, so it is good to know them and think of them, that a man may take as many as he can." And here is a site with more or less everything we ask for, yet we shall not take it. We are both decided: it will not do. And this time what offends our excessively pernickety palates is the flavour of private privilege.

Certainly the hills are beautiful. Rising grassy slopes crowned with beechwoods. Yes. But the slopes are not farmers' fields as we thought at first, but paddocks with horses for hunting. And the woods are private woods, with pheasants for shooting for all we know. It is not that we object to the blood in blood-sports, we object to the sports. We like farming country. It was one of the stipulations. I have forgotten who said that of all country sounds they found the cry of the cock-pheasant the most offensive. And the most offensive sight? Hunters in paddocks perhaps, but she did not say. (I think it was Elizabeth Bowen.)

In England nearly all the old villages are sympathetic. They may not be the picturesque treasures of guide-book standards, but they generally have the friendly cheerful air of an independent community life. The few villages I actively remember as

places where I would not willingly live are those huddled at the
gates of some local big house. It is not that they are poorer than
others, or the villagers oppressed. The nearness of the big house
no doubt provides them with extra work, and with a conscientious landlord who can afford to build them bathrooms and
mend their leaking roofs. But somehow such protected villages
do not welcome us with the irresponsible cheerfulness of more
independent groupings. We are conscious always of the unseen
house behind the park wall. There is an indefinable sense of
oppression. Is the village street in too restrainedly good taste
perhaps? Do we only imagine, or is it true, that village voices
never rise above a certain discreet level? Certainly there is no
open horizon, but only the uncompromising boundary wall
which encloses a different way of living.

It is not that I pity the villagers. I should object to living
inside the park wall almost more than outside. The wall is a
defensive barrier, not against animals but human beings. It is a
division, and the two sides are not fundamentally friends. The
implications are equally unpleasant whichever side we see them
from.

As William and I considered the surrounding countryside
from our new site, we were both conscious of a growing park-
wall feeling. Not that there was the slightest shadow of any wall
in all the miles of open view. But nonetheless we thought we
could sniff the faint but unmistakable smell of private privilege.
When we walked in the woods we came on discreet little notices
here and there whispering PRIVATE. There were fences—not to
keep animals in, so we suspected, but people out. Nor did we
like the look of the horses, well-groomed horses in well-fenced
fields and never a sign of a farm.

It is a shame, poor things, when horses are such handsome
creatures, but I do not like them. For me they are too much the
perfect evocative symbol of a great many things we have no
intention of living with, on either side of the fence. Swift might

feel that his horsy Houyhnhnms were the ideal race, but I never have—though it is not the horses themselves which I mind, but the attitudes they generate in the human beings who sit on their backs. The conjunction of man and animal was harmless no doubt when a horse was merely a form of transport (it is still alright when the man is a little girl and the horse is her pet), but modern adults are not at their best set up on top of horses. The additional height of legs has an undesirable influence on the human personality. That motor-cars have an unfortunate effect on character is commonly accepted, but horses I think have a worse. Even on wheels man is preferable, and on his own two feet greatly superior to any four-legged state. Modern man is not intended to be the top half of a centaur, except perhaps in circuses.

And in the fields round our new house there are quite certainly too many horses. Not an odd one here and there, lovingly cared for by the farmer's daughter, but half-a-dozen lordly together, sleek with that labour of grooms which gives to all but professional race-horses so arrogant and unsympathetic an air.

This is not where we want to live. Both William and I are silently decided. There is nothing to say. It is over. In practical affairs we may not always agree, indeed we long ago found that the smoothest way (the only way) of working together is simply to divide our spheres of operation and add together the finished results. But when it comes to sniffing an atmosphere, to knowing how we feel about the intangibles, then we seldom differ. We seldom even need to explain our reactions, for we react together.

The view, the sun—everything is perfect. But we will not live here. We don't like the horses.

❖❖❖❖ *9* ❖❖❖❖

"The severall situations of men's dwellings are for the most part unavoidable and unremoveable: for most men cannot appoint forth such a manner of situation for their dwelling, as is most fit to avoide all the inconveniences of winde and weather, but must bee content with such as the place will afford them."

It is the beginning of Parkinson's *Paradisus*. A wise voice and a disillusioned, the counsel of a tolerant man who knows that we live by compromise. We must be content, he says, with such as the place will afford. He might have been writing to warn me off Thoreau three centuries later. Men cannot appoint forth the situation for their dwelling, but must bee content. And we have not been content. We have turned down all manner of situations for dwellings. And if Parkinson knew he must compromise in an age as innocent of planning and overcrowding as the seventeenth century, surely it is purest folly in the twentieth to hold out so obstinately for perfection. There is no reason to believe that there must be an ideal site waiting somewhere if only we can find it. Even my blind optimism cannot always preserve me from doubt. It is quite possible that what we are looking for simply does not exist. On the bad days I foresee us, after years of searching, left with nothing at all but the bitter regret that we did not compound for the next-best when we could still have it.

In all the two-year effort from first restlessness to removal-day, this is the worst time of all. There will be others more trying but none so despondent. And the family are no comfort; this is my concern not theirs. I provide houses: they live in them; they are perfectly comfortable in what is already provided. As for the new being better than the old, they have no opinion either way, most males being quite incapable, as far as I can see, of imagining any place to live in until the walls are solid round them and the roof over their heads. Certainly my three are. I am dragging them all from a house they live in without complaint, and am setting them down, so they seem to feel, bleakly exposed on a houseless hill-side. And all to satisfy some whim of my own which they are not in the least concerned with.

But as to that, I shall take no notice. Unless the housewife stands firm on her own domestic territory, the household never thrives. However I can scarcely expect them to rejoice in being uprooted, even though the roots dragged up are mostly not theirs but mine. And I do see that it must be trying to live with my alternate exhilarations and despairs. It is trying for me too, and I long for a cowlike state of emotional indifference. If this is feeling more and more about less and less, whoever would want to be a disciple of Henry James?

The stormy forties. All through our young adult state we are warned of the coming intensities of the forties ahead. It is a kind of barrier reef, so people imply, which we struggle through to the calm beyond. But the forties are not so much a time of emotional storms as emotional reorientation. Or so I no doubt prematurely pronounce from my half-year's progress into this much-discussed decade. Of course there are storms. But there always have been, they are part of the climate I live in. Emotional storms, self-generated. But they always were. And they are not so much storms as an emotional temperature violently plunging and soaring between despair and exhilaration. But it is nothing to do with being forty: it was the same at twenty.

Nonetheless, even in this first introductory year there is a strong sense of milestones, of leaving one phase of life behind and beginning another. But the leaving-behind is in no way a sad relinquishing: it is rather a getting-rid of old responsibilities, a getting ready for a fine new beginning. In most women's lives the high tide of effort is bringing up children, not only physical effort, but also meeting the constant emotional demands of a family in active development. Even in the most equable of houses, which ours is not, the task of the parents is less like cooing over a nest of agreeing birds than steering a ship through a stormy channel in a high wind of change.

But now, so I feel, the most strenuous part is over. The boys are almost grown up and increasingly independent, and the household no longer has to be reorganized every few years to suit their fast-changing development, but is run-in to a settled routine of four more-or-less adults living together. There is more time—not only more physical time, but more emotional time, which makes far more difference. There is no longer the same urgent need of nurse and mentor and judge and disciplinarian—all the priggish and unsympathetic rôles which a family lays on the parents' only half-resigned shoulders. There is no longer the constant necessity for a sacrificial family buffer between the warring moods of emotionally different individuals. It is time they managed alone. They must make their own mistakes, must learn to quarrel and come to terms by themselves. From now on the crises will have to be increasingly grave which will bring me out on to the family stage in the old heavy cast-off rôles. I shall be myself now. I too shall have moods to consider. For the private emotions of mothers are overruled by the long discipline of their children's needs, and moods are a luxury which housewives cannot indulge in, being too concerned with managing other people's.

After the long restricting routine of family life I am now suddenly free to be selfish. I can sit in my own room and arrange the flowers on my private window-sill, and hug myself with a secret sense of delicious guilt. There are few states of mind more satisfactory on every level than justified selfishness.

But my new leisure is not for arranging flowers, not at least until we achieve a window-sill of our own to arrange them on. For despite the checks and disappointments I still mean to move us. I am dull but determined. Though I realize now that building the house we want is going to be like providing an ambitious meal with the raw materials strictly limited, and that what we lack in materials I must make up with extra time and effort. And even my time is limited, for besides the London household and practice to run with a minimum of help, I must turn out and clean through the Regency Villa ready to sell it. And the more we can sell it for, the more we shall have to spend on making our new house as we want it. It must therefore be put on the market as attractive as I can make it.

One of its virtues as a house when we first moved in was the vast amount of storage space. But now I consider it with dismay. Not only cupboards and scullery and room-size pantry, nor even the whole area of the house under the roof, but outside too are a gardener's room and coal-house and apple-store, and a whole row of non-descript sheds. And now the whole lot are full of rubbish, the cast-off litter of living. For storage space is always full—it is one of the natural laws. Without the space we throw away the rubbish as it comes, and never need face this seven years' accumulation which now overwhelms me.

For I am no cheerful Hercules for the clearing-out. My reaction to the ordinary mess of living is not cheerful bustle but a growing depression, and faced with the whole of this house to clear, I sink despairingly. As hay-fever sufferers are allergic to harmless pollen so am I to the normal squalor of human living. They sneeze, I despair. I long to live like a cloud which from no matter what foul damp of polluted water still condenses out as purest vapour. But human creatures live in their own pollution, in the rubbish which has filled every undisturbed hollow of this house like silt from the stream of our occupation.

Fortunately the boys are immune to my depression. Indeed there is nothing they like better than going through attics and cupboards and sheds in search of discarded treasure. And since the garden has plenty of space for bonfires, we burn the discarded rest in a blazing triumph of getting something done at last. We are burning our boats as well as our rubbish. There is no question now of staying, for even if we never build our new house we shall certainly leave this one.

So in the time left from London I get the Regency Villa ready to sell. In the time left from that I look for a site. As the spring grows to summer our week-end meals become steadily simpler. The food in casseroles changes to eggs and bacon, and quite soon I imagine, the eggs and bacon will be cooked by the people who eat them and not by me. As for the site-hunting, I have less time, less energy, less optimism, and must make up for all three by greater determination. We have left one house (for the change is now irreversible) and unless we find another we shall be homeless at the end of our London lease.

Every search has its own momentum. It is why a search makes such an excellent plot for a film or story. The beginning is often indeterminate, a vague drifting towards our goal through the distractions of other affairs, as it was with the earliest idea of our changing house. It was what we would do in the unspecified "later on" which lay ahead. But once started on any search our interest grows irresistibly and crowds out all other preoccupations. The pace quickens. It is as if we had started to move down a gentle slope which now grows steadily steeper. It is like being drawn into a whirlpool, or coming within range of a magnet whose power is more compelling the closer we get.

Not that I am resisting the slope. On the contrary I am running downhill as fast as I can pelt, considering my domestic impedimenta. The week in London, the week-end in the country. But as the summer goes on the week-ends encroach on the weeks. When the daylight lasts all Friday evening there is no need to wait till Saturday to travel out. I speed up my Friday working-day to have everything packed and ready when the family come home in the evening, and as soon as the rush hour is over I whisk them off for supper in the country. The credit for all is an extra Saturday morning for country affairs, the debit for me alone is that Friday is now as exhausting as Saturday and Sunday.

But the week-end has long ago ceased to be a pleasure. It is a burst of intensive effort from which I recover during the slightly less intensive London week. I discipline myself to a week-end routine. Before I go looking for sites I must do my home-work. I must first see that the garden is mown and tidy (the others will mow the grass, but they first need catching and en-couraging, and for anything else but simple mowing they are no use at all). Then I must turn out and get another area of the house ready to leave, for I deal with the house in limited doses like taking medicine. So the garden, the house, the meals ar-ranged for, and then I can go, but tired now, and unexpectant, and much troubled by the thought of the good sites we have so improvidently turned down. After all, the country we want will have to be protected by *something*. We must be reasonable. Yes. But still not by horses. I will go on looking.

Plodding by now is the only pace I am capable of, and if I had not seen our destination so enticingly in the visionary begin-ning, I should give up the effort and enjoy the summer instead. For this is a whole season lost. The spring has meant nothing at all but the year nearly half gone already and no site found, and this lush early season of summer means only that the lawns need cutting more often. The search is now so obsessive that I feel every moment in the country is wasted unless I am site-hunting. The door is closing—I feel it more urgently every week-end—and unless we slip through soon we shall be left outside for ever. I now begrudge not only the time spent gardening or turning out rubbish, but eating and even sleeping. Any time in the house at all means frustration. As for the countryside, it only exists in terms of what I am looking for. So do my human fellows. Cer-tainly I have never talked to so many country people in so short a time: not only every friend and acquaintance I can think of, but farmers and shopkeepers and postmen and milkmen and lorry-drivers, old men sweeping roads, strangers I meet in villages, farm-labourers laying hedges in the long-ago winter, and householders leaning on garden gates now it is summer and warm.

But the conversation is always the same—Do they know of any land? etc. etc. As contact with my fellows it is as limited as a tune played all on one note. And by now the family are quite simply bored. Even if I invited them they would no longer spend Sunday morning looking at the sites I found on Saturday afternoon, and even if I found a site I would not ask them, and anyway I find no sites—it is weeks since the last.

I too am bored—and disheartened and tired, and we have scarcely even begun. When I think of the long-drawn-out effort ahead I sit down overwhelmed in the nearest field and wish I had never started. But we are now so thoroughly uprooted that I shall have to do something. To settle back again in the Regency Villa would be as unsatisfactory as getting back into a tepid bath we left half an hour ago.

At the end of the war a doctor once told me that he could always tell without asking which of his patients had spent the war as civilians in London and which in the forces. For the civilian war was so much more exhausting than the mostly inactive active service, that civilians, so he said, always looked ten years older than anyone the same age from the forces.

When our house is built I also shall look ten years older. I may even of course *be* ten years older as well unless we make more progress than this. March has gone, and April and May—a wasted spring of the not inexhaustible store. And now it is June beginning, June of soft nights and the grass in flower.

March, April, May, June. Lovely. For in all the English language there are no words more evocative than the names of the months. They are not simply dates on calendars but the very quintessence of poetry, and to say them through is to summon up in procession all the changing seasons of the country year. "It won't be ready till March," someone says, and the sky shines clear and delicate as it does in early spring. "In July," they say, and the fields blaze with poppies and the dust is warm along the edges of lanes. September is calm and gold, October's "O" holds great blustering gales and the trees new-stripped to their beautiful branches.

But shall I be looking for sites when the trees are bare? I wonder. I sit dejected in fields which are neither in-filling nor rounding-off, and feel my life stream away in wasted springs and wasted effort. The others are content as they are. Why can't I be still and enjoy the summer? Is it worth it? Since a search has its own compulsion irrespective of the quarry, we may well become so obsessed with the search itself that we no longer judge the value of what we seek. Is that what has happened to me? Surely it would be simpler to persuade myself to contentment than to rehouse all our lives only for my insubstantial reasons. It is mere restless folly to fret. I pay out my precious life for airy fancies. June now. It will soon be mid-summer. A whole lost season. And why am I doing all this? For nothing. For Hecuba. Only for one view rather than another framed in the living-room window.

⬦⬦⬦⬦ *10* ⬦⬦⬦⬦

We have found our field. In June with the hedges a celebration smother of wild roses. The final field this time (no more false alarms), where the house now stands facing full to the mid-day sun. This time there are no hesitations. The positives are so overwhelming that they crowd out even the possibility of negatives. We have found our ideal site at last. It is rather absurd after all.

We always get what we want, so the philosophers tell us, if we want it intensely enough. If we look straight ahead and put boldly to sea then good luck will join us. So they say. There is no such thing as luck, they imply. We simply create our own opportunities by our own insistence.

I have never known whether the wise men offer this as a conclusion from facts observed, or only as a subtler modern philosophical statement of the old-fashioned God-helps-them-etc. style of exhortations. I only know that I looked for our field and found it, and that it not only fulfils every one of our unreasonably exacting conditions, but even offers further excellencies we never thought to ask for. And since any description would choke in superlatives, it is necessary to write out the facts as a list:

The view—Perfect the whole way round the 360-degree horizon.
The sun—Exactly where it should be.
London—Thirty-five miles of uncrowded roads.
The station—A mile away in the village.
Services—Along the lane.
Neighbours—Along the lane and out of sight but near enough, we trust, to count for in-filling.

As for the intangibles:

Protection—By public not private bodies.
Occupation—Farming and forestry.
Horses—Only one in the miles of view. A small kind of cart-horse with reassuringly shaggy legs.

As for the further unlooked-for excellencies:

A high hill against the north winds.
Welcoming woods on the other side of the lane.
A deep hedge between field and road, grown through

years of neglect to an impenetrable tangle of flowers and shrubs and trees.

And as if in confirmation that here at last we have found, not the Promised certainly, but anyway the Hoped-for Land, the grass is scattered this first summer evening with the strange greenish lights of glow-worms.

But there was no doubt from the first moment I scrambled through a gap in the hedge and discovered the unguessed-at panorama beyond. Here it was. Quite simply that. Everything we wanted. No doubts this time. No questions or calculations. Only the unmistakable conviction of ultimate excellency.

Even William and the boys are convinced at last. I fetch them to see, but tell them nothing, only show them the gap in the hedge. They scramble through, then stop to stare, for the view is a sudden and overwhelming confrontation which no one could take for granted.

Yes. Oh, yes! A long appreciative gaze round the whole lovely circle of the horizon. William looks at me in astonishment.

"I never dreamt this was the sort of thing you were looking for. Whatever made you think you'd find anything like this? It's superb. There can't be anything better in the whole of England. If we had a house here I can see that I'd begrudge every single day I spent anywhere else."

At last William's six-month-long indifference has warmed to enthusiasm, and for the first time since we started he is eager to move.

"But what makes you think this field's for sale? And even if it is, how do you expect to get permission to build?"

But these are questions for me to concern myself with, not William. The family has been and approved (the boys are as emphatic as William), it is my task to change accepted intentions into accomplished fact. And even their approval, though emphatic, is brief. They have gone back home and left me to rejoice alone with the view.

I am standing in a medium-sized field enclosed by hawthorn hedges. Along the lane between here and the village there are houses. Through the hedge on the far side I can just make out the roof of another single house along the lane beyond, so surely this can count as in-filling? On the other hand the house is an alarming distance away, and clearly there must be some limit to how large a gap can be called in-filling, or any open country would qualify between here and London.

I must not be too hopeful, I warn myself sternly, or this time the disappointment will be more than I shall recover from. But it is here or nowhere. Either we build a house on this particular plot of earth or we stay in London. So I must make the needful inquiries calmly, as a routine detached from feeling, and must ask them like a Latin exercise in questions expecting the answer No.

But I have no real doubt. We shall build a house and live here. I am certain. If the house already existed I could hardly be more emotionally convinced. However it is still very far from existing. We have not yet even made any progress except the satisfaction of our exacting fancy in the way of sites. Between the Yes—Oh—Yes and the solid roof over our heads there is a vast amount to be done, and the starting-off is threatened by three most formidable questions.

Is the field for sale?

Can we afford to buy it?

Will the planners let us build if we do?

I suppose everyone when faced with an array of difficulties has his own particular way of dealing with them. The prudent start with the easiest and gradually work up to the hardest, but I would rather get the worst over right at the beginning. I choose the hardest and do it first, and with that safely achieved the rest is easy. It needs only one real effort and the rest scarcely counts, for the large cancels out the small. It is like diving all at once into cold water instead of walking in gradually and feeling the cold creep horribly up our back.

The worst difficulty about our field is the building permission. So I will start by seeing the planner again. An exchange of letters. An appointment arranged. A Sunday evening when William takes the boys back to London and leaves me to my Monday-morning fate.

I walk into the office with an alarming sense of my heart in the balance, and wonder if this is how young men used to feel when they went to ask the loved-one's father for his daughter's hand in marriage.

We sit down opposite each other. He is urbane and non-committal as before. The same man in the same office, but a very different me.

"Do you remember I came to see you some months ago about building a house?"

"Yes. I remember."

"And you told us about in-filling and rounding-off."

"Yes. I remember."

"Well we've found a site that we like and I've come to see if it can count as in-filling."

(There it is. Out. The suitor has stated his case—I love your daughter. Will you let me marry her?)

He reaches for his map in ambiguous silence. Will I show him exactly where?

I show him.

Certainly, so I reassure myself, he can't deny that the field is a gap between houses. There they are on his map with their gardens exactly shown. But equally, alas, I can't deny that compared with the gardens on either side the gap is most ambitiously *large*. He considers it and says nothing.

"It really is in-filling," I urge, but doubtfully, for his silence alarms me (as the fathers' silences must certainly have alarmed the hopeful young men).

"What exactly do you want to build?"

(It is like asking the prospective son-in-law what his income is.)

"We want a modest sort of house," I tell him, "with a garage, and perhaps a summer house. And a largish garden."

"The field is seven acres," he says by the way of answer.

(My daughter is used to living in comfort. Can you support her at the standard she's used to?)

I had guessed the field was something like that, but didn't find out since I hoped it was smaller.

He looks at the map and I look at him. It is very quiet and the sun shines in through the window.

"There are other sites in the area," he says at last. (My daughter is not the only girl in the world.) "Sites already scheduled for building. Have you seen this one? and this?

He points them out on the map and I think how he never mentioned them the first time I came, and how much effort it would have saved if he had. However, by now I know them as well as he does.

"Yes. We've seen them all. And a great many others as well. But none of them are right. This is the only one exactly what we want." (For it is no use Father suggesting other young women we might marry.)

"Why do you want a field of seven acres?"

"But we don't. An acre is plenty. If we can have just a piece of field that will do. We only want to live in that particular valley."

"Yes," he agrees, and his voice is no longer guarded. "It's a perfect place for a house. One of the loveliest bits of the country anywhere around. I've walked up there dozens of times over the years and I never get tired of it."

I restrain a tremendous urge to jump up and shake both his hands. It is the turning-point not only of the interview, but of our entire house-building fortunes. I know we shall have our site. It is not that he has said anything to make me suppose so, but no one talks to another person in such friendly fashion if they intend to do them ill. Our enemies gloat when they deny us, our friends are shamefaced, but when kindly people share our enthusiasms, then all is surely well. (It is as if Father had smiled at the young man and said, "Yes. Isn't my daughter a dear?")

But smiling is not agreeing. He is looking at the map again.

"Seven acres. What would you do with the rest of the field if you built a house on an acre of it?"

"We would fence it off and let a farmer have it for grazing."

"Are you sure of that?" He looks at me hard. This is clearly a crucial question. (It is as if Father suspected the young man of bigamy.)

"You're quite sure you've no idea of putting up other houses besides your own?"

"Certainly we're sure. We only want a house for ourselves in the country. We're completely selfish. It's exactly because there aren't any other houses that we want to be there in particular. We'll let the field to a farmer and have cows for nearest neighbours."

"One thing. If you did build your house there we shouldn't be bothered with any more applications. You're not the first by a long way to fancy that plot you know." (It is Father resigning himself to losing his daughter and accepting (*surely* accepting?) the most insistent of her many suitors.)

"Besides, I can see that unless you get somewhere to build you'll be sending us in applications for years to come."

I say nothing to interrupt so promising a monologue.

"Well," he says, and I know that the interview is over, for people used to interviewing can dismiss their visitors by the faintest change of inflection. "Well. I can't really help you. It's not for me to say. I've no personal powers at all. These are Council decisions." And so on and so on.

It is the kind of two-part pronouncement divided by a "but," where the first part only qualifies the second, which is the half that really matters. He can't promise *but*. "But I see no reason why you shouldn't put in an application to the Council and see what they think."

(It's not for me to decide for my daughter. I'll have to consult her mother as well, but I'll certainly put it to her.)

But no young man can have felt more confident of his future wife that I of our house, and the sun is a blaze of triumph like trumpets as I walk out into the street. This is England of the compromise and the non-committed. We are promised nothing, but. . . . But I know when it's safe to be hopeful.

Years ago I once knew a Polish refugee who had fled his persecutors and reached England destitute and bewildered. Driven by desperation he overcame his ingrained fear of all officials and went to the authorities to ask for help. He poured out his long story of misery. They listened in silence. They made notes on sheets of paper. He was a carpenter by trade, he said. He was learning better English. Could they find him a job? Was there anywhere he could live? Would they promise to let him stay in England and not send him back to arrest?

They said nothing. They made more notes. They asked him a great many questions. More notes. No encouragement. Despair. For what had he gained by leaving his whole life behind him and fleeing to England? He had merely exchanged one wretchedness for another. He now had a dossier in a government file in a foreign country as well as his own. The horrible game of cat and mouse would start all over again.

Very well—so they dismissed him. They would see what they could do. They promised nothing but he should come back tomorrow.

Knowing nothing of English "buts" he gave up all hope. Authority had simply got rid of him by the usual putting-off methods, and tomorrow they would probably arrest him. And he described to me in Polish-style English, made even odder by the intensity of his feeling, how he passed the night in such black despair that from hour to dark hour he wondered whether to make an end of the struggle and be done with it.

But the Poles are a tough race and he was young. Next day he went doggedly back. There was nothing else to do. He had nothing to lose. He waited his turn on the bench in hopeless apathy.

Ah, yes. Would he come in, please? They were expecting him. They were glad to say that they thought they could help him.

And just like that—so he told me with undying astonishment —they produced for him everything he'd hoped for. They really meant it. It was all arranged. A job and a family to live with. Lovely people. He lived with them still. He was incredulous with joy. He was still incredulous years after when I knew him.

But since I am not a Polish refugee but have lived with the English all my life, I know that if authority sees no reason against what we want, then it is already half-promised. In our cautious English idiom we state our positives by negatives which cancel out. We shall get permission to build.

◇◇◇◇◇ *11* ◇◇◇◇◇

But what use is building permission with no site to build on? For the field is not ours. This may be a more tractable difficulty than the planning but still it is very real. Every time I climb through the hedge I am trespassing, for our treasured field belongs to somebody else who has no idea in the world of what we are planning to do with his property. Emotionally it may belong to us as entirely as Traherne's world did because he loved it, but that, alas, is not firm enough tenure for building houses. In everyday non-metaphysical practice we don't know who owns our field, nor whether they will even consider selling it.

I pick a spray of late roses from the hedge (*our* hedge) and sit in the grass, which is half flowers like an alpine meadow, and consider who the official owner of our domain might be. A farmer perhaps, for there is a row of hen-arks across the bottom, and the amiable rough-looking horse over the hedge might well belong to a farmer's small daughter. But certainly not a very efficient farmer, for the hen-arks are empty and broken-roofed, and though I may prefer grass to be half flowers, I doubt whether dog-daisies and blue speedwell are the best of grazing. Besides, there is the gap. No sensible animal would stay for five minutes in so unpromising an enclosure. It is all very hopeful. If the field's only use to its owner is growing wild flowers for trespassing strangers, then he may be glad to be rid of it.

I ask in the village. The village is vague. That seven-acre field up the hill? (Country people describe fields by their acreage.) No. They don't rightly know who owns it. They can't rightly say. One time, of course, it went with the farm across the valley. But not now. Not no longer. Got rid of it after the war. Not worth the working. Though it did once carry a crop of barley they recollect. Weren't too bad a crop neither. Not considering. But poor land. No heart in it. The soil's too hot and too shallow.

But I don't want to know about barley-growing. I want to find the owner. Well then, I should ask in the pub down the lane. Sure to be someone there who can tell me.

The owner of a field in the country is not hard to trace, certainly not a field with hen-arks. When I eventually find him he is half-farmer half-retired-army, and I go to call on him at the week-end. But I am now so confident in our progress (this is the advantage of getting the worst over first) that I take his agreement for granted, and the visit is a matter of form rather than trepidation. No. He doesn't particularly want that field. Poor land. More trouble than it's worth. Yes. He might consider letting us have it. But what do we want it for?

"They'll not let you build if that's what you're after. Very tight they are, about all this area. I'd have put up some houses on it myself if they'd let me. Plenty of space for a dozen or more and each with a nice bit of garden. Got it all planned out. But they wouldn't hear of it. Not they. Wouldn't even listen. Very obstructive they are. You'd think you'd a right to do as you pleased on your own land—but not a bit of it. You can't so much as knock a nail in nowadays without asking their leave first. Goodness knows what this country's coming to." (Clearly he has not come to terms with his "They.") "So if it's house-building you're after you're wasting your time—they'll not let you do it."

Perhaps not, I say. But we're applying for permission just the same, and if They let us build a house, will he sell us his field?

Well, yes. He supposes he might. He wants less work now he's older, and he's getting rid of his chickens in any case. He can't see any reason why he shouldn't let us have it. But all the same, we're wasting our time (a final rumble of discontent). Very tight they are. They'll not let us build. Not They.

So there it is. We shall get our field. The search is over at last. And what I must now do is settle down thankfully and learn to be patient through all the intolerable delays I already foresee ahead. They are starting already. It has been a searching spring and now it is a negotiating summer. Agents, solicitors, forms, interviews, more forms, discussions, forms in triplicate, more interviews, maps and plans for more authorities than it seems possible could take an interest in one modest house in a quiet country lane. There is no doubt that our proxy conscience is insisting on all the facts before it gives its approval.

And every stage of the proceedings brings new difficulties and delays. One wall climbed over never reveals a clear road ahead as I never stop hoping it will, but only another obstruction to slow us up. Our forms in triplicate miss the Council meeting. The owner of the field will not decide on a price. The Council considers our application. The owner has doubts about selling. We must get permission from the land-use people for building on farmland. Unless I can learn to be patient I shall never survive the summer.

But it is only impatience now: all doubt has vanished. The delays and difficulties are merely annoyances which never reach my inmost conviction that we have found our perfect site, that in time a house will be built and we shall live in it. And no doubt anyone used to negotiating would have known beforehand what to expect. But I am not a negotiator, I am an arranger. I am used to making up my mind, but not to having two sides in the proceedings.

Fortunately William is better than I am (*far* better in fact, for my standard is clearly not high). He stays calm and takes risks as I never do if I can help it: I hate to take risks, even with a good chance of winning. By now William is reassuringly involved in the proceedings, but still by my standards most diplomatically self-controlled. He wants the field. Yes. But still he is heart-whole about it, as I am not. He deals with the owner. He is self-assured and non-committal. They agree on a price. It is certainly more than for farming-land but equally certainly less than for building. It is more than we hoped but less than we feared. And after all a seven-acre field is more than we hoped as well. We shall be landowners almost.

We *are* landowners almost. For it comes at last, permission to build a house in our chosen field, only provided we agree to certain conditions.

We must buy the whole field.
We must build one house only.
We must not build shops.
We must not build a factory.

Searching. *Where?*

We must not dig a lime-quarry.

We must not do any of the other unlikely enterprises we might be secretly intending. Some of the conditions are so very surprising that we can only wonder what bitter experience lies behind them.

But the field is ours. I can sit in it now with perfect propriety. It is our own hedge now where I pick, not June roses any longer, but their red autumn hips, and ripe blackberries, and the curiously sophisticated pink and orange spindle-berries, which even after years of familiarity I never find growing wild without surprise. We own a piece of the countryside now, however modest. It is all we ever wanted, and far more than we need to put down roots and feel we belong. And now that the field is safely ours I can describe it at last without fear of committing my heart as a hostage.

It lies along a lane winding up into the hills about a mile behind the village. The road runs east-west on a ledge along the side of a shallow valley, a gentle hollow ringed with hills rather than a valley proper, and opening out westwards to one of the several gaps through the Chiltern scarp. The field lies south of the lane, an oblong stretching along the road-side and screened by the neglected bosky hedge grown high with young trees. The 550-foot contour line runs exactly across our seven acres, which are tilted to the sun and slope easily down to meadows and hedges below. On the facing hill-side wide arable fields divide up the gently rising slope, and the hedges flow in curving patterns over the shapes of the land. The opposite hill-tops are a mile and more away across the hollow, rounded shoulders of chalk half-wooded and half-wild, and pink over all summer with a shoulder-high forest of rose-bay willow-herb. At the head of the valley to the east the hills curve round in a circling sweep like the rim of a bowl, and this continues behind us in a steep slope beginning abruptly on the other side of the lane and rising sharply another 250 feet to the hill-top. This is the edge of the Chiltern scarp, here facing north across the Vale of Aylesbury, a reassuringly solid mass between our southern slope and the winter winds.

As for the view—any description would sound an incoherent rapture. It stretches round us on three sides in a wide unbroken sweep of flowing hills encircling the shallow hollow with its gently rolling floor, and in this oval saucer-shape we are half-way up the edge. The land-use, as the planners call it, is the farming we set such store by. Admittedly the farmers tend to have distinguished ancestors like Charles Darwin and Henry Fielding, but it is farming nonetheless—hayfields and cows and hawthorn hedges and the changing patterns of ploughing and harvest. And the woods which give the hill-tops their sense of mystery and wildness are not private property but part of the Government's Chiltern Forest: young plantations of beeches mostly, inter-planted with pines and larches to nurse them up into the tall and noble beech-woods of the chalk-hills. Here and there by stiles along the hedges there are notices: not inhospitable park-wall warnings of PRIVATE, but the green-painted Buckinghamshire signposts pointing firmly to PUBLIC FOOTPATH. And where a track leads into the woods there are melodramatic and highly coloured warnings against starting forest fires, exuberantly leap-ing flames with crude black trees silhouetted against the red, all done in some old-fashioned style of coloured enamel.

For miles on either side of us the hills are unenclosed country open to everyone; woods and thickets and the short-turfed downs of the chalk uplands. The whole area is crisscrossed with the PUBLIC FOOTPATH kept open by the signposts and by care-fully marked dotted lines on the one-inch Ordnance maps. But kept only technically open, for in this motor-car age not enough people now walk along country footpaths to keep them free of the spreading briars and brambles and willow-herb which border them, and most of them are half-lost in a green and flowery tangle. For this is the final, the most astonishing virtue of our astonishing site.

Searching. *Where?*

The country is beautiful and unspoilt.

It is less than an hour from London (not by one train a day but by dozens).

It is open land and welcomes all comers.

No one comes.

PART THREE

PLANNING.

WHAT?

12

"FOOLS BUILD HOUSES FOR WISE MEN TO LIVE IN."
So far no one has liked to speak out quite so bluntly, not at least when we could hear them, but a great many people have implied it more or less unmistakably. It has come to be my test between the sheep and the goats, though even when they are sorted out I have never known which of these much-divided animals are supposed to be on the side of virtue. But I know very well which category I warm to of those who discourage us with wise saws (*and* modern instances, for most new houses seem to be tales of woe), or the fellow-enthusiasts who listen to our building-plans and can scarcely wait to rush off and build a house for themselves.

"An officious Adviser is one of the unwelcomest Guests that can come to many Persons, what Occasion soever they may have of it." Yes. He is. And unwelcomest of all of course when we are most in need of the advice. Fools build for wise men. It is nasty, knowing, unimaginative, predatory, sly, inhuman, and mercenary. And I shall not listen. But still it is a saying with enough of the conviction of truth to undermine anyone's confidence, and it undermines mine.

Certainly we would be glad to live wisely in a house built by someone else if only we could find one to fit. After all we have tried out a fair variety of second-hand houses already by living in them, and none of them has more than approximately suited us. We know very well from experience how awkwardly our particular lives fit into houses built by other people for other ways of living. And even if we did find the right house by some chance of twin domesticity, there is still the other and equal problem of being in the right place. If the small chances of either are multiplied together, the hope of finding the house we want in the place we want is too remote to be worth pursuing any longer.

But clearly the implication of folly has upset me, or why should I justify our house-building at this advanced stage? It is too late to doubt. We are building a house to suit us, and we shall have no one to blame but ourselves if it does not suit us exactly.

It sounds very simple, but we are astonished to find how difficult it is to start off like this with nothing at all to steer by. I keep being uncomfortably reminded of Wordsworth complaining of the unexpected difficulties of living in "unchartered freedom." It is easy enough to plan alterations to a house already lived in—I have altered in fancy dozens of houses to fit all kinds of lives. (It is a way of passing the time when bored.) But it is very much harder, we find, to build a house from the start with no mistakes to need alteration. And architects, even the most understanding of brothers, are less help than expected, for in their different sphere they are like the planners—positive certainly, where planners must mostly be negative—but still they have a kind of aesthetic conscience to hold the balance between the different attitudes to building of the observers and the users.

People who commission buildings mostly know what they want. They may be mistaken of course, but they are generally quite definite about it. Use has its determined and interested supporters always. But beauty is a much less straightforward matter, depending on judgment and taste and such like imponderables, dangerously insubstantial qualities to weigh against the solid facts of what its inhabitants want a building to *do*.

Of course there are blind theorists who simply equate use with beauty—a question-begging doctrine like believing that virtue is its own reward. But it is years now since the true-blue functionalists flourished (they believed in exposing the plumbing as well as the floor-joists I remember), the evidence against them being everywhere so overwhelming. Good design is never so simple, in architecture or anything else. It has to be planned for by architects whose first concern with a building is what it looks like. It is why they can whole-heartedly admire fine buildings, even when as completely unfunctional as the eighteenth-century mansions which moulder so magnificently in the damp English farmlands like three-dimensional stage-sets. For if any bedazzled young architect believes they were ever habitable even for their hardy eighteenth-century owners, then he should listen to Duchess Sarah on Blenheim, and read Horace Walpole on the miseries of staying at Stowe.

It is what is the matter with our Regency Villa. It is no more than an infinitely distant poor relation of such grandeur, a cousin dozens of times removed, but it belongs to the humble end of the eighteenth-century tradition, and it still inherits too much of the family character for us to live in it comfortably. It is built mostly for visitors, not occupants. First the paved veranda with its roof and railings, then a hall with arches, and a quite unnecessarily spacious staircase with three windows and ornamental bannisters, and a sunny landing the length of the house. The drawing-room is large for the visiting Joneses, but all the rest cramped and sunless, and the bedrooms mere boxes, as Dr. Johnson complained at Kedlestone. Far too much of the house is wasted in entrance and circulation, impressive and draughty journeys from one uninviting small room to another.

Which is only to say that it does not suit us. Other people may live in it and find it to their liking, and certainly it might suit a more formal life than ours. But as a container for our way of living it does not work. The eighteenth-century mansions were splendid boxes built in terms of the boxes, and the human contents had to adapt their lives to fit them as best they could. But we do not fit, and our villa does not work. Its proportions are wrong. Not wrong on the drawing-board—not a matter of balancing the masses and spacing the windows and doors—all of which is no doubt excellent. But the life it was built for is wrong for us in the twentieth century, and proportion is a matter of the right size and placing of units in lives as well as in buildings.

For buildings are shells which enclose human living, and should therefore begin with the vital activity, not with abstract dimensions. They are organic structures secreted by the life of the organism they shelter, and architecture is surely the art of building containers for living which enhance the life they contain. Not which make life easier or more efficient—no mere machines for living or working—but buildings that enhance our experience of the human state by raising the life they contain to a higher intensity.

But I protest too much, like the Lady. Pages and pages. And chase after theories, and gallop off on hobby-horses. And most protest is mostly tiresome. And hobby-horses are not for serious travel.

But it is not protest so much as justification. For we too care greatly what buildings look like, yet we are going to put up a house which no architect will ever consider anything but dull. And the inhabitants? Certainly that is a different matter. For whether they are there for a day or a week or a year of all the seasons, the inhabitants live in it with notable and reassuring satisfaction.

But this is out of time. It is justification by hind-sight. For though I may be sitting in the finished house and writing a book about it, the house in the narrative is not yet started. Not even designed.

Architects know about building houses.

Housewives know about living in them.

Co-operation is therefore essential.

But will any architect co-operate with so opinioned a housewife as I am? It is fortunate that I have an architect brother who will put up with our unreasonable demands. Or at least I hope he will: I must be careful. But before we ask him to do the designing, we must first decide what we want designed. What exactly do we want our new house to be like if not like the old one?

I think back to all the various houses I have seen and coveted. They are an odd selection when I look at them critically, from a row of barns scarcely converted from cows to humans, to the mansion Robert Adam built at Kenwood, a cosy and cheerful and habitable house which refutes all my eighteenth-century criticisms. But most of my houses are in no way distinguished, and some of them are so very far from what any architect would approve of that the kindest word to describe them is nondescript. Yet one thing they all have in common, the one essential test for me of any house—I can imagine a family living happily inside them.

Very well then; a house for a family to live in. For our particular group of four people to share without friction, and combine in to everyone's satisfaction.

But this is a far more exacting specification than it seems, for although in our peculiar way we might count as a united family, we are certainly not united by our similarities but rather by our unfailing interest in each other's differences. The new house will not be a setting for a homogeneous group like the comfortable domestic households I always envy, but rather a container for four different separate units held together by some complicated interaction of opposites. We each have our individual tastes and interests, and we are none of us particularly tolerant of anyone else's. One likes Palestrina played very loud on the gramophone, another likes jazz played equally loudly. One likes to read in solitude, another to talk. One likes tidiness, one likes mess, the windows open, the windows shut, bright lights, dim lights, large rooms, small rooms, a bungalow and a high house with upstairs and attics. No wonder we have never found a house to suit us, as this one somehow miraculously must.

One thing is certain. It must be a house of firmly sealed-off separate rooms where we can each live our separate lives when we want to without either causing or suffering disturbance. For us there can be no open-plan houses, and in any case they seem to me just as much architects' follies as the eighteenth-century mansions. It is the old question of looking-at versus living-in, which is even more acute in small houses than large. The problem is clear:

The smaller the house to live in the more important the separate sound-proof divisions.

The smaller the house to look at the more important a single unbroken space and bother the noise.

There is no denying the dilemma. But how can anyone live in a house where whatever anyone says can be heard by everyone else? What happens when the two gramophones are on together? Or if one person must have silence to work when another has invited friends for the evening?

But architects seldom wait for the answers. They may build beautiful open-plan structures for others to live in, but they themselves mostly go off to the separate-compartment houses which are essential for anything but public places.

Not that the trials of open-plan living are anything new. Such hotel-style houses already horrified Henry James generations ago.

"The universal custom of the house with no one of its indoor parts distinguishable from any other is an affliction against which the visitor has to learn betimes to brace himself. This diffused vagueness of separation between apartments, between hall and room, between one room and another, between the one you are in and the one you are not in, between the place of passage and the place of privacy, is a provocation to despair which the public institution shares impartially with the luxurious 'home.' To the spirit attuned to a different practice these dispositions can only appear a strange perversity, an extravagant aberration of taste." And his objections are typically Jamesian, that the open-plan loses "the essence of the room-character, that room-suggestion which is so indispensable not only to occupation and concentration, but to conversation itself, to the play of the social relation at any other pitch than the pitch of a shriek or a shout. . . . It takes a whole new discipline to put the visitor at his ease in so merciless a medium."

But *we* need no warnings from anyone. We know that our family could only live in an open-plan house by one chosen member privately murdering the other three and living in it alone. (Though even murder, I suppose, could never be really private.)

It is not that we are particularly unsociable. One of the reasons indeed for so insisting on divisions is that we all have separate friends and visitors and phone calls (I must remember the telephone somewhere with a door to shut) and that it is intolerable if we all have to share each other's social life whether we like it or not. Certainly there must be space for the entertaining we all share, but that is much simpler to achieve than privacy and quiet, which have to be carefully planned for. "The highest luxury of all" (it is Henry James again) "is constituted privacy." Separate rooms then; the first fundamental. But what else?

Most houses are introverted: it is the natural condition of a dwelling. They are the personal shelter we come back to from the impersonal world outside. When we come indoors we pass from public living to private, and until we go out again we are indifferent to what goes on beyond our own small enclosure. So most houses are self-centred, inward-looking. Their consciousness is contained within the walls which contain their physical life.

But we want this house to look outwards. We shall come here not to be indoors but in the country, and the chief preoccupation in any room will be the view outside the window. We do not want a house which shuts us away from the countryside, but only which shelters us from the weather. We want windows everywhere, uninterrupted sheets of glass as invisible barriers, and the vistas through and across the house aligned on the windows. And on the ground-floor glass doors opening straight to the garden, so that in summer they can be set wide and the house will be an outdoor living-space only roofed over by the bedrooms above like a canopy.

It is not a house that any true country person would live in for a moment. People who work in the country see quite enough of the outdoors, and when they come in they like to feel enclosed and intimate. Country windows are small, and even so they are thickly screened with curtains and hedges of geraniums. The working-day outdoor world is kept firmly outdoors where it belongs. But we come from a city, and the country will not be our work but our pleasure. The house must look outwards.

Then what else do we want of this most extrovert of houses? One thing essential is peace of mind. Until William retires we shall mostly use the house for week-ends and holidays, and we must therefore be able to leave it empty without concern. For if when we are away from a house we are nagged with worry for the possible harm it may come to, then the cost is too high and we are better without it. From years of such divided living I have learnt the lesson thoroughly. Any house we have in the country must not depend on our help to see it through the uninhabited week, and especially through the uninhabited winter. And of all the possible kinds of house there are only two which can be lived in intermittently without worrying about the intermissions. One is the expendable and the other the self-supporting.

The expendable house is the cottage we find for a song, and camp out in for summer week-ends and holidays. During the winter we shut it up and leave it to survive till spring as best it can. And if one year the winter proves too much for its increasingly feeble old age, then never mind, we are only a song worse off, and the summers have been worth the singing. But the cottages in country near London are not expendable: they are quite shockingly expensive. To buy them with a song it would have to be a prima donna's gala performance, and we certainly cannot abandon them to the hazards of winter.

The other house is the self-supporting, built to look after itself and comfortable enough to use in all weathers. The roof must be leak-proof, the walls damp-proof, the plumbing frost-proof, and for the comfort of the human beings inside, the heating must be simple enough to warm a room in half-an-hour from arrival on cold winter nights.

I can assure potential week-enders that these are not benefits common in the houses they will be offered. For that matter they are not common in houses of any kind. Tudor farmhouses will not do (the plumbing freezes) nor Regency Villas (the roof leaks under snow) nor houses like the one in London, where the high rooms are not noticeably warmer at the end of several hours' fire. (Though neither, for our comfort, are they noticeably colder after a week-end without. But that is only because our neighbours have central-heating, and the boiler is against our wall.) Besides, all houses before the twentieth century were built without benefit of damp-courses, and left unlived-in they moulder like corpses.

So a self-supporting house. What else? Surely the others must have ideas about what they want. I will ask them.

"The view," they say.

"Yes, yes. But go on. What else would you like. Now's the time to say or never."

I wait for their answers, but I waste my time. One wants an *enormous* swimming-pool, the other a garage fitted up as a laboratory for experiments, and "Why can't the car stand outside like it does in London?" William has set his heart on a flagstaff with a flag for his birthday and will offer nothing else. And I too have my private fancies, especially a long-cherished plan for a glass extension to the living-room filled with orange-trees in tubs and with little bright singing-birds, and for their perches black marble heads of Roman emperors half-hidden among the leaves. I have plenty of other ideas too, most of them even less useful, but I shall keep them to myself, and shall equally give up asking the family for theirs. And I think perhaps I won't mention any of them to my brother. He is likely to be discouraged enough in any case. For all we are offering him to work on is a list of incompatibles—rooms large enough for parties, small enough for two people alone. An airy summer house and a warm winter house. Open vistas and closed spaces. The list could go on indefinitely—the users' list for living-in, for no one as yet has even mentioned design.

But I think we will let him find out the difficulties for himself. They will scarcely be hard to discover. We will invite him down to see the field, and fortify him with view before we begin.

⬦⬦⬦⬦ *13* ⬦⬦⬦⬦

It is autumn, and I sit among the purple knapweed and sweet-smelling marjoram of our neglected field, and rock with such a passion of impatience to live in the house which I now feel

vividly round me that I wonder how I shall survive the long
delays of the building ahead. It was never worse than this, not
even when I was a city child longing for our rare seaside holidays, and in the weeks before we left, every conscious moment
was such an endless trance of waiting that I used to worry
whether I should live long enough to survive the eternity before
we set off.

> "I must hear from thee every day in the hour,
> For in a minute there are many days."

Juliet knew all about impatience (though I once heard someone ask if it was a misprint). But the house, not the red-herrings.
The plans. For we are no further on yet than my arrangements
of rectangles on the backs of envelopes.

"I have written in a small piece of paper sundry other notable things," said Leland in his *Itinerary*. And so have I, but I lose
the small pieces of paper. However my plans do now at least
include a staircase, which perhaps counts as progress.

In any case much of the planning is already dictated by the
site. If we want sun and view for every room, then the south
front must be an uninterrupted row of windows, and the business of living (what I call the oddments and my brother the
services) must be arranged along the north side looking uphill. It
will give us a long narrow house, which is also the natural shape
for this hill-side, ledging into the slope on a terrace along the
contours and parallel with the lane. The north side of the house
will be the public side facing the road—garage, entrance, staircase, and all the oddments. The south side will be living-rooms
looking straight out across the valley, a view undisturbed by any
fidgety foreground of domestic to-ing and fro-ing. The rooms
we live in will be overlooked by nothing at all but the sun,
which is just as well since the south side of the house will be
mostly windows.

So far it is simple. It would be deliberate perversity to
wrench so natural an arrangement to any other plan. But how

are these rooms with a view to be arranged? If we want the effect of an open house but also separate compartments to live in, how do we propose to combine them? However it is visual openness we cherish, the noise and warmth we want sealed into separate enclosures, and glass is wonderfully obliging in doing both. So what if we use glass doors for the communal parts of the house like the staircase and entrance and kitchen, and align them on windows so that we look straight through the building and out into the open country? And if we use wider glass doors to divide the living-room, so that although with them open it is big enough for sociability, yet part can be closed off for William and me alone on winter evenings? And if we make the bedrooms big enough to use as private sitting-rooms as well as sleeping-places? And certainly the kitchen must be large enough to be dining-room as well. For now that the hostess is also the cook, why dish up food and carry it to cool from one room to another, when she can serve it effortlessly hot straight from the stove it is cooked on? So the kitchen must be large, with a table in the window for six or eight people, and a glass door to over-flow into the garden for summer lunch-parties in the sun.

But the *kitchen*, not the parties. It will have to be on the north with the bathroom and lavatory I suppose, to keep all the plumbing together. But what about the sun? And the view? For I will *not* have this working heart of the house in a cramped sunless corner as it was in the Regency Villa. I care about kitchens. Not kitchens with stainless steel and electrical machinery, but kitchens to live in. For I long ago realized that a good kitchen makes more difference to the life of a household than any other room in the house. To the household in general, not only to the housewife cooking meals for a family and friends who join her to help and talk. All the family use a kitchen. With its sink for water and cupboards for tools it is where all the odd jobs of a house are done. The kitchen table is a makeshift work-bench for all sorts of home industries. It is where we sew and

draw and spread out maps, where we make out-of-hours coffee
and sit and talk, where we consult the *O.E.D.* (always at Sunday
lunch) to find what akimbo comes from, and tit for tat, and
willy-nilly, and loop-hole.

In most modern servantless households the kitchen is the
natural centre and should be given the best position in the house.
In other rooms we are mostly preoccupied or asleep, but in a
kitchen we are actively conscious of our surroundings, and their
quality here matters more than anywhere else in the house. The
shape of our kitchen bowls and jugs affects us more intimately
now than our china tea-cups. The texture of our kitchen floor
makes more difference to our day than the drawing-room carpet. And since modern design is far better at elegant use than
elegant ceremony, twentieth-century kitchens can perfectly
well be as satisfying as eighteenth-century salons, since each of
them is the room where the essential life of the house belongs.

But most modern kitchens are no more part of the house
than the bathroom is. They are little-used, gadget-filled cupboards where the housewife grudgingly shuts herself up to work
alone for the least possible time. It is an old-fashioned conception of domestic life derived from the household with servants,
where the family lived leisurely apart, and the servants minis-
tered to their needs out of sight in the kitchen quarters. The
only change is that the lonely housewife now replaces the com-
pany of servants. No wonder she revolts, and the cooking
suffers. Since modern households are servantless, in-and-out, do-
it-yourself, wife-with-a-job units, houses where only the woman
is expected to use the kitchen are as obsolete now as houses where
the mistress was never expected to set foot over the kitchen
threshold.

So a heart-of-the-house kitchen. But the sun? Certainly the
plumbing must be on the north, but since the house is long and
narrow, why not an L-shaped room at one end, with the sink in
the north arm and the table in a window on the end wall, either

east or west? There are views both ways which it is a pity to lose by having no windows to see them from, and either direction would get the sun for half the day, as well as a view of the sunny hill-side in the north-facing windows. Better on the west perhaps, since our late-rising city habits give us only four hours or so of sun before mid-day, but the whole of the afternoon and evening. The kitchen then at the west of the house with sunsets for supper, and the garage and entrance at the east, services on the north, living-rooms south. We progress. I draw it out on one of the envelopes I always carry now in my pockets. It makes a shoe-box-shaped house, which does well enough, though it does look rather large, even when cramped on the back of a small envelope. But never mind, we never intended a cottage.

But is that the sort of thing we mean? my brother insists. He must know what we want from the start, otherwise he'll waste everyone's time designing the wrong kind of house. We must tell him exactly.

Yes. But there is no need for him to insist. I am sure we shall tell him far more exactly than he is bargaining for.

My poor brother. For his architectural standards will be hindered at every stage by our unshakable conviction that our practical lives matter more than his abstract proportions. In designing a house to suit us he is likely to feel less like an architect than a tailor asked to make a coat to fit a sprawling figure who has no intention in the world of standing up straight, but only of sprawling more comfortably. He will be given a long list of essentials, most of them incompatible. He will be expected to reconcile all this with the practical business of building walls and holding up roofs, and combine it into a whole which will satisfy his very proper architect's desire to produce a good-looking building. I doubt whether our share in the arrangement will seem to him like either co-operation or compromise. But still, we can try. It can hardly be worse than finding the site, and look how successful that is.

Planning. *What?*

Yes, look. For we hold our planning discussions out on the field in this gentle autumn weather, and across the valley the trees are half-dark, half-gold in the sloping afternoon sun, and the sideways fall of the light reveals subtle modulations on the smooth grass slope of the opposite hill.

Yes, says my brother. But the *house*. He sees more or less how we want it arranged, but what do we want it built of for instance? And what kind of roof?

As to that we have only one condition. It must need no maintenance during our lifetime.

The English have various national peculiarities, particularly about their houses. For an Englishman's house is not only his castle, but also his pride and his care, and quite often his justification as well. A great many English houses seem to be there, not for the benefit of the inhabitants at all, but for their own architectural pleasure. The owners are servants, and the house accommodates them for its own well-being, not theirs. An odd arrangement, yet it seems to work, for many houses are the loving preoccupation and chief lifework of those who live in them. And certainly it suits the houses, for much of the charm of our country towns and villages is in houses cared for and cosseted by the resident care-takers who happily imagine they own them.

It is a form of symbiosis which suits many people, but it does not suit us. There are too many other things we want to do, and if I had cared to keep a house alive by transfusions of my own life-blood, we would never have left our Tudor farm. For of all the houses I have lived in it is the one I have most loved, and certainly the one most in need of a human life to preserve it.

Leaving it empty was like leaving a dearly loved and defenceless friend to drown in a steadily rising flood, when by our staying we could have held back the waters for at least a lifetime. I guarded it through storm and frost, mended its wiring and plaster and plumbing, and greeted each spring with distemper brushes to cover the patches of winter damp on old walls with no damp-course. I watched like a mother for leaking roofs and cracked drain-pipes and damp floors—all the dangerous signs of serious ill health in houses. I nursed it for years, but now I want a house which will look after its own healthy self without me. I no longer want to use my life guarding any building from decay. For disintegration is in the very air that houses breathe, and from the moment they are built their state is a gradual abandonment to destruction. But then so also is mine at forty, and I now want a house which will shelter *me* from the cold and rain instead of the other way round. If we build a new house it must need no mending of any kind for the next fifty years. (We are firm on our fifty now, for surely in this green setting we shall live to a green old age and sit in the sun reading telegrams from the Queen on our hundredth birthdays.)

It is one of the few really practical reasons for building—that in our old age we can sit back in perfect confidence that even if we do nothing at all to the house for twenty years together it will come to no harm. My time now is precious and I long for the much-maligned twentieth-century push-button living. Not so that I can play with my household gadgets, but so that I can forget them. For years I lit fires as our only heating and cooking, and I never again want to do more than turn a switch to warm a room or boil a kettle. And I want everything simple: austere if need be, but bought at the lowest cost of my attention.

For we begin by collecting treasures, we surround ourselves with the beautiful, the choice, the rare, the precious. Or we would if we could. For luxury, so we feel, means living elaborately among fine things. But what we don't know in this acquisitive beginning is that fine things are paid for twice over, once by the effort to acquire them, and from then on indefinitely by the attention to preserve them. (It is like the fat losing weight—they can never give up the diet.) And a surprising number of luxuries are within reach of anyone willing to pay for them with sufficient preoccupation. But I am not prepared any longer. I have reached the stage now where luxury is not in fine possessions but in carefree possessions, and the greatest luxury of all would be the completely expendable.

So we want a house which needs no attention. It is our single condition, our one bid for luxurious living. But single condition or not, it seems to impose most drastic limitations. It is no use admiring photogtaphs of elegant airy structures half-glass and half-wood-panels topped by an invisible flat roof. There is no flat roof we can afford which will not need maintenance before we die. *Long* before, so we are warned by those who should know. It is no use imagining we can put on a flat roof and forget it, so they most earnestly assure us. And forget it is exactly what we intend to do—forget the leak-proof roof and the rot-proof floors and the rust-proof windows and the frost-proof plumbing and the solid brick walls—no wood-panels to oil nor rendering to paint. And the shape of the house must be compact and simple, with no projections to cut off the sun and view, and the least possible outside walling to leak away inside heat.

Poor architect. For what he is reduced to is a plain rectangular box with brick walls and a tile roof—a depressingly old-fashioned way of building for a modern young man, and one with its own strict rules of construction. I can scarcely expect him to be enthusiastic, and certainly he is not. No house will look right he protests, with half the walls glass and a great solid roof at the top.

No. I know. But we shall be living in the house underneath the roof, not outside in the garden looking at it. And once underneath the only thing we shall care about any roof is whether it leaks.

But because we should be whole-heartedly on his side if we

were anyone else but the future inhabitants, I feel we must justify ourselves. If we were building our house in a town, so I tell him, then it would be different. In a town, I concede, houses matter more from the outside than the in, and the pleasure of the thousands of people who see them every day outweighs the convenience of the few inside them. In a town we would not interfere (though this seems unlikely, as we both of us know, and he looks at me sadly). But this house will be invisible from everywhere but our own garden, or as a distant shape from the opposite hill-side so far away that no roof will show either heavy or elegant.

I expect him to say there is no opposition between the inside and outside of buildings, that a good-looking house is a good house to live in, and so on. But he says nothing. For after all here we are, as anxious as he is for a different roof if only he can find one that works.

And while he is considering such practical details, will he use wall-surfaces, I ask him, to conserve all the possible heat? And will he have windows tightly fitting without draughts? And since in positions as sunny as this, glass lets in more heat than it leaks out, all the south windows as large as the walls will allow and still hold up the roof? We want surfaces everywhere very simple, without ledges or mouldings or corners for dust. Everything as plain and solid as he can make it. And everywhere built-in wardrobes and cupboards, and whole walls of shelves for books and bits, and deep window-sills we can sit on. No. Lower than sitting—almost to the ground, so that sprawling in low chairs or lying in bed our view of the outside world is uninterrupted.

"Yes. Yes. Alright." (He interrupts the flood, and no wonder.) "But we're a long way off window-sills yet. Still, you've given me plenty to start on. *Plenty*," he adds ruefuly. "I'll make out some sketches and see what you think."

Planning. *What?*

◇◇◇◇ *15* ◇◇◇◇

The end of the year is busy with a long succession of letters backwards and forwards, telephone calls, sessions with plans and slide-rules, and catalogues of windows. When we started the leaves were still green in the beech-woods across the valley, but before the first tentative plans are ready for judgment the woods are already changing to gold, and on the telegraph wires along the lane the swallows sit in twittering rows like black beads loosely threaded on looping aerial strings.

But here is the house defined on paper at last, a bespoke building tailored exactly to fit our family figure. It may not be a house to delight architects but it certainly delights us. It has all we asked for and more besides, all kinds of extra delights provided by my brother as it took shape on paper.

But isn't it rather large? Even drawn out at a quarter of an inch to a foot it does look quite an ambitious sort of house. Of course we could use it all comfortably now, but what about later on when the boys leave home and week-ends are no longer a succession of school-friends to stay and friends out for Sunday? How will it suit two people living their private lives?

These are questions which every family house must answer sooner or later. But if the house we want now is twice the size of the house we shall want later on, then the arithmetic is not very difficult. We can build it as two separate living units, use them both now and only one later on. With careful planning it should be possible. There are two entrances, so a door to seal off the hall and staircase would make a self-contained first-floor flat. As a single house it will suit us excellently now, for a staircase door is an extra barrier against noise and, even more important, against the ground-floor warmth streaming off up the staircase (the Regency Villa has been a traumatic experience in all our lives, not only mine). And later on we should have a separate flat for visitors, or married children perhaps, or to let and pay off the mortgage if the weather turns rainy days.

But I wish I could keep my mind on building the house instead of daydreaming of life inside it. Is this what we want? But, alas, that is not the relevant question, for whether we want it or no, we can certainly not have it. It might well be our perfect house except for one insuperable disadvantage—it is far, far, too expensive. After even the briefest of consultations with the builders there is no doubt at all. We can't possibly afford to build it. Whatever anyone may pay us for the Regency Villa it will certainly not be enough to raise the walls of this house more than half-way to the roof. So we mutter about cutting our coats to suit our cloth, and other such wise and discouraging precepts, and start the planning all over again.

We take out half of the beautiful double living-room, and since this means losing an extra room at the back to correspond and two rooms back and front on the floor above, that is four rooms less at a single stroke, which surely must make a difference.

We take out the central-heating—another impressive slash. And fortunately the autumn is mild, so we grieve for its loss less feelingly than we might. But we tell ourselves we would rather be cold than cramped, would rather wear jerseys indoors than not have room to move. Besides, the gap is so alarmingly wide between the builders' price and ours that we shall only cross it by heroic economies. We make all the rooms a little smaller (it is a pity we are all so large) and we give up various luxuries like sliding windows and teak in the kitchen. And while we sit tightening our belts on paper, the beech-woods smoulder to muted orange in the autumn sun, and the last of the restless swallows leave for Africa.

The second plan is a modest house, but it still will not do.

Planning. *What?*

Tightening our belts is not enough it seems, and the next move is cheese-paring.

But if so many things we want have to go, we must make no mistakes about the things we keep. What about William? What does William care most about in the house we are building more to please him than me, since I am only half but William wholly convinced he wants a country life? What does he want to keep of our now limited choice? Will he think about it seriously and say?

But William is never serious about the domesticity he regards as my wifely concern. He can't arrange the raw materials of a house as a setting for living in, nor even imagine a way of living which does not exist. But what does he *want?* I insist. He must have *some* ideas. Do I really want to know? he asks. Well then. He'd like a sunken marble bath with steps going down and gold dolphins for taps. And a pretty, plump, barefoot girl to paddle round and clean it. That's what he's always wanted, he says. And a sound-proof room lined with cork, like Proust's. And of course the flagstaff. Quite *seriously* the flagstaff. He really means it.

It should count to my credit at the end that I never once lost my temper, but only swallowed hard and promised myself silently never to ask again. And the boys? (This is their last chance too.) The boys' new fancy is for walls that sink into the floor all round when they press a button. But what about holding up the roof? I ask. "Oh," they say airily. "That's what architects are for. Didn't you know? To hold up the roof without any walls. If it's going to have *walls* we can design it ourselves and don't need an architect."

One thing then is settled for good. No more consulting except with my brother. From now on announcements only. The problem then: to plan a house we can afford which will give us the best possible value in living.

To reach a central level we can either climb down from the

top or up from the bottom. We have tried climbing down and have not got low enough. We must start from ground-level.

So. A house. With rooms. Not how many rooms do we want, but how few can we do with? We have cut out four already, can we take out any more? Not William's study. But the spare bedroom? No. We must keep the rest. But can we make them smaller? Since they will never be visually cramped with one wall glass, it is only a matter of space to move.

In every house there is a certain amount of essential furniture, less in the East it seems, but a great deal in the West—chairs, tables, beds, cupboards, shelves, drawers, wardrobes—a bulky array which Westerners find necessary for the business of living. And all this bulk must somehow be fitted into the rooms we inhabit, yet must still leave space for us to move about and use it. If our rooms are small we can abandon inessentials (standard-lamps can be wall-lamps, chests-of-drawers can also be bedside-tables, and why do we need a table for plants when the window-sill will do?). But there still remains an inescapable minimum (we don't sleep on our Western floors nor kneel round our tables to fit in somewhere, and this we generally do by reducing the floor-space left free to move in. But as a way of economizing on the size of a room it has obvious limits (chests-of-drawers, for instance, are of doubtful use if the drawers can't be opened). The proportion of furniture to floor-space varies in ordinary houses from about one quarter furniture to three quarters space, which is pleasant, to half each space and furniture, which is almost unusable in rooms we live in. (Chairs in particular need a surprising amount of floor, either pulled in and out at table or lolled in by the long-legged.)

So I work out our minimum needs on a scale like the Japanese system of six- or eight- or ten-mat rooms. Yes. Even with Western furniture a ten-mat room is big enough either for beds or for living. We can shrink the rooms a little smaller. We shrink. Reckoning the building at so much a square foot our economies are promising. But still not enough, so what next?

Planning. *What?*

As a household shopper I long ago found that the best value in a range of goods is nearly always the quality one up from the bottom. The lowest grade sacrifices too much to economy, the higher grades are too much concerned with luxury. But the first grade from the bottom starts with the barest essentials and adds the most important improvements, the extras which are the best value for the least extra cost. So we will build our house at the first level up from austerity.

The leaves are falling in soft russet showers from the beeches, which will soon be austerely bare, and the house too must be stripped of every expendable luxury. There are many things we can do later on when we recover from the original building, and I strip them out ruthlessly. The floors can be left concrete and covered with matting. The built-in furniture can wait. The walls can be simple white-wash for the first few years, and so on and so on. (A covered porch from the entrance to the garage is a sad loss, but better to keep the glass extension to the living-room, even without its Roman emperors.) And there are some things we will not alter. The foundations must be as solid as we first intended, the construction as sound. We are not prepared to sacrifice a single inch of glass. It is easier to line rooms with bookshelves as we one day hope to, than to knock out a hole in a supporting wall to enlarge a window. So we will keep our extra-wide doors and plate-glass windows.

The autumn is over before we have finished, with the mi-grant red-wings arrived for the winter and calling musically as they fly overhead and settle in the berried hedge along the lane. The hedge behind the house, I almost said, for to me the house will scarcely be more real when it stands there defined in solid bricks. And this time we have managed to meet the builders on more or less the same level; like tunnels converging from differ-ent sides of a mountain which must somehow meet in the middle.

We are ready now for the plans to be drawn up in detail and sent to the planners for approval. Not that there is any question, for in this plain oblong house built of bricks and tiles there is nothing even the most conservative of planners could object to. It is only a matter of filling in forms and waiting.

But what about the architects who seem to be quite a large proportion of our friends when I stop to consider? "Houses are built to live in and not to look on: therefore let use be preferred before uniformity except where both may be had." I can quote Francis Bacon at them if need be, and they will probably never remember that he spends the rest of his *Essay on Building* describing an elaborate palace designed entirely for looking on. But no one could fail to see that we have preferred use before uniformity, and whatever theorists may believe about the identity of Form and Function and suchlike capital-letter abstractions, it is *not* a way of designing which produces houses particularly handsome from the outside. Kitchens and bathrooms and lavatories and coal-sheds and dust-bins and yards and garages do *not* make the best of entrance-fronts however well they are screened and assembled. It does *not* make the most interesting elevation to have all the rooms in a row with no projections to cut off the sun or the view. Windows arranged as the best size and position for the rooms inside do *not* necessarily emerge as the best for the outside façade as well. What we have asked our architect to do is assemble a lot of boxes for looking at the view, and we are delighted with how he has done it. He has designed us exactly the house we want to live in, and as for the outside—it may be dull but it is certainly not ugly—and we care not at all for conceptions like "entrance-fronts" and "first impressions." We *like* the kitchen door conveniently flanked by dust-bins and coal-house. We like the entrance next to a covered yard for changing muddy boots and leaving wet rain-coats. We like to walk in through all the unconcealed business of living in the country—it is why we come out from London.

Henry James, as a discriminating critic of European life, considered that the particular gift of the English was for living in the country: "Of all the great things that the English have invented and made a part of the credit of the national character, the most perfect, the most characteristic, the one they have mastered most completely in all its details so that it has become a compendious illustration of their social genius and their manners, is the well-appointed, well-administered, well-filled country house."

There. And all in a single well-administered well-filled sentence. But the country house must be built to suit the social manners of the people inside it, and the lives of twentieth-century country-dwellers are much less well-appointed than anything Henry James foresaw. And in any case *we* are not concerned with producing an illustration of the English genius, but only with whether this house will suit our modest version of country-living. Certainly it is planned as a shell to house our life as the organism inside, but have we predicted the future organism accurately enough, or is there some dreadful mistake which once built into bricks and mortar will be with us for the rest of our lives? How can we know till the house is built? But we must either change the plans now or change our living to fit the established house.

Through years of packing for family holidays I long ago found a method for making sure that the luggage we took covered any possible development of the holiday. I simply imagined the life of the packed-for through every kind of day, and put in what was needed. Hot weather or cold, walks in the rain, days in the house, untidy days on the beach, more-or-less tidy outings to local towns. I even, so natural is pessimism in mothers who take children to cliff-top cottages for a month, put in bandages and sedatives and the minimum sick-room equipment of toys and books.

It worked excellently for holiday packing, and perhaps it will work for this house as well. I imagine a day from getting up to going to bed. A day in summer with doors and windows wide and the garden one with the house; or in winter warmly enclosed in our draughtless air-locked container. A day by ourselves; or with friends for supper; friends for the week-end; the boys' friends for the weed-end (a quite different category: Is there a room sound-proof enough from the rest of the house for making and retreating from noise?). And inevitably the days in bed. What will the bedrooms be like as sickrooms? Are the window-sills low enough to lie and look at the view instead of the usual cracks on the ceiling?

Yes. As far as I can see the house will work for all the permutations of family life as we live it. It will suit *us* then, but will it suit all the other people who will live here after us? For a house built as solidly as this one will survive us by centuries, and a long succession of generations will live in it when we have gone. Will it suit them as it suits us? Will it still be the kind of container a family will want for domestic life a century from now? There is no way of telling. We only know that the species which become obsolete are those which become too specialized and are therefore unable to change to suit changing conditions. And this house is essentially unspecialized. It is a group of adaptable room-units for constructing a setting for living in. For half-a-dozen different settings for quite different ways of living within the same four walls. And no one can surely be expected to do more than that for the needs of an unknown posterity.

◇◇◇◇◇ 16 ◇◇◇◇◇

Will we decide where we want the house? So the builders have asked us. For what we should do before winter, they tell us, is hire a bull-dozer and get the site levelled straight away, so that it can consolidate (it is their word, not mine) in the next few months of bad weather, firm and ready to start building in spring. They have given me the name of a firm which hires out bull-dozers complete with drivers, an old-fashioned firm they say, as if that must be recommendation enough to satisfy anyone.

I ring up the old-fashioned firm on their new-fashioned telephone and explain what we want: a long narrow terrace levelled along a hill-side.

"How long?"

"That depends how long it takes. Room for the house anyway, with level space round it."

"What's the slope like?"

"Quite steep," I tell them. "I don't know exactly."

"Then you're going to need a good wide terrace if you want to be comfortable."

"Yes," I agree. (Certainly let's be comfortable.)

"What's the soil like?"

"Solid chalk."

"Is there space to turn a fair-sized machine?"

"All the space you like," I assure them.

"And the gate to the field?"

"A farm gate—eight feet wide I should guess."

"Fine," they say. "That all seems straightforward enough. You decide exactly where you want the house and just let us know when you're ready."

"Fine." I catch their confident manner. "That's fine." And for the first time in all our proceedings there seem to be no difficulties of any kind.

I wrap myself up in an enormous anonymous family coat (it is almost winter) and go up to the field to consider. I am joined by a dog, a large black Labrador too fat for its size. It is friendly and curious and joins me now whenever I come to the field. I sit on the grass and look at the view: it sits beside me and looks at me. But this can scarcely count as entertainment even for the least demanding of dogs, and it seldom stays long after the first routine greeting and inspection but goes off again through a gap in the hedge and leaves me to my meditation.

Will we decide on the site? So simple and so important. For there are many things we can alter later on if need be, but the position of the house is clearly not one of them. It must be settled irrevocably now, with no second thoughts.

The main decisions are simple: we want the view and we want the sun. But which view? And how much sun? For we can vary the angle of the house to the hill-side, we can set it higher up or lower down the slope, to one side of the field or the other. I have sat about all over the hill-side in these last few months, and every time it is a new discovery how the least change of position alters the view in a quite astonishing fashion. Even twenty yards up-hill or down changes the whole relationship of valley and hills. Twenty yards to one side or the other composes the distance with a quite different foreground.

Then there is the direction. The slightest change of angle frames a completely different outlook like a picture in the windows. So that a yard up-hill or down, a few degrees difference in angle will decide for ever the relationship between house and valley. So which view exactly?

There is the eastward circle of flowery hills at the top of the valley, or the expanse of meadows below us rising to the wooded slopes on the other side, or the long outlook to the west across the gap in the scarp to the blue hills beyond. Since an unbroken sweep of fine country surrounds us on every side, should we simply build the house at the highest part of the field to take in the widest possible range? Or would it be better lower down, where the slope levels off and gives a view backwards as well— of the great round hill shaggy with young beeches and hazels and pines, and crowned with the earth ramparts of an Iron-Age camp and its majestic ranks of full-grown beech-trees? The view, we all say. But *which* view? It is not a question of knowing which we want, for we want them all: the difficulty is to resign ourselves to choosing one and giving up the others. Not that we shall lose them entirely, for there are the west-facing kitchen, and various small windows at the back of the house. But these are prospects we shall look at, not places we shall inhabit as we shall the countryside framed in the living-room windows.

I ask the others but I waste my time as usual.

"We've told you already about disappearing walls, and if your brother can't manage that, then he can build a revolving house and we'll choose our view every morning and press the button. Or of course we could have the house on rollers and pull it round the field to a new place each spring. They do in America, you know."

I silently reaffirm my resolution not to ask anyone else's opinion. But what would *I* like? For unless someone decides to accept the limitations of exact definition we shall admire our view for ever houseless on the hill-side.

The slope of this side of the valley is a general falling-away to the south, but the field also has a very slight superimposed valley of its own, a wide shallow hollow running down-hill, but so slight that it shows only when the shadows of the sun are low across the field. If I had not spent so long here already at all hours of the day, I should never have seen it; but one evening as the sun went down, the sideways illumined grass was slowly darkened with a shallow band of shadow running down the slope. All the field was gold in the setting sun except this slight hollow which the light could no longer reach. Perhaps it is the course of some long-lost tributary stream which once drained the melting snow from the hill-top when the ground was still frozen after the Ice Age. But again, perhaps not. For amateur geology is mere ignorant and unprofitable guessing, and in any case the hollow is too wide and shallow for a stream. It is as if a finger had lightly stroked wet clay.

I went to look at the large-scale map of the area and there it is, a slight swerve on the 550-foot contour line which crosses the field. And here we will build our house, looking down this scarcely discernible hollow. And we will face due south and have all the sun we can. For the twentieth century worships the sun as it no longer worships the newer gods, and in England the sun is a divinity whose presence never overwhelms us: it seldom even satisfies us. So we will gaze full into the noonday sun, and if the house gets too hot in summer we will open the windows. In hot summer weather we shall live in the garden in any case.

We can now stake out the site of the house. Even to the others it is something of a ceremony, and for me it is triumph. I have borrowed my brother's measure, found four old cricket-stumps the boys long ago discarded, and their equally discarded cricket-bat to hit them in with. We will mark out the plan. I stand at the top of my now invisible hollow and the boys measure out the house-front each side of me. Two stumps hammered in for the two front corners. So. Then back up the slope with the measure (I know the size by heart without a plan) and two more stumps to complete the rectangle. There. The house. I am glorious with achievement. Even the roof going on will be no more a definite stage than this. The house is started—we have laid the foundation-stone of the operation.

But the boys are bored. If there's nothing to do but look at four cricket-stumps in the grass then they're going home. But there is something else. I want them to help me work out how steep the slope is, so that I shall know how high the bank will be behind the house and how deep the drop below the front terrace.

For some curious reason the slope of a field marked out by four stumps looks very much steeper than a slope without. Quite surprisingly steeper, for though the field seems a gentle slope the stumps are at two very noticeably different levels. But we shall soon know exactly how different, for I have thought out an every-man-his-own-surveyor way of measuring the fall, and the boys are at exactly the age to enjoy this kind of semi-scientific ingenuity. I have no idea how slopes are really measured, but if we prop a plank level and measure the drop we can surely work it out. In the back of the car is a six-foot plank, a pile of bricks, a spirit-level, a ruler, a pencil, and paper. In the field are two boys eager to help as they have never been in all the proceedings till now. There is nothing I need do but sit and admire.

They choose a patch of field and lay the plank down the slope. With one end wedged in the grass they prop up the other on bricks until the spirit-level on the top shows exactly horizontal. Then they count the bricks and work out the sums on scraps of paper. It is all rather absurd, and I am sure there must be a less laborious method, but none of us can think of one, and as it is the boys are most flatteringly impressed by my fore-thought.

The slope from back to front of the house is one in ten, so they announce at last, and the field between the house and the road varies from one in ten to one in eight where it climbs to the road. They seem perfectly confident of their calculations and it seems a likely figure, though rather steep I should think, for cars on snowy mornings.

But the boys are going home now. It is cold they say, why don't I come too? But anyway they'll expect me for supper—so they tell me twice over, knowing quite well that I shall be driven home long before supper-time by the dark which is gathering already in the angles of the leafless hedges.

But I care nothing for housekeeping anywhere now except in this shadowy house-to-be. This is reality and all the rest mere unavoidable distractions. Here is the house. Here we shall live. The fact that for everyone else but me it lacks roof and walls and even foundations is of no importance, no more than a temporary matter of a missing fourth dimension, soon to be provided. This is the real beginning which for me already includes the end.

⬦⬦⬦⬦ 17 ⬦⬦⬦⬦

I ring up the firm of excavators again and tell them we are ready as soon as they like to start.

Next week? they suggest. On Wednesday?

How long will it take? I ask, mentally crowding the work of the London week into a furiously busy Monday and Tuesday.

Two or three days, they expect. It all depends on the weather, and how much work we want done. They might have to finish off on the Saturday morning if they run into any snags.

Wednesday then, we agree. At ten o'clock on the site; for since the bull-dozer's steel tracks tear up the roads, it must first be brought by carrier from another job.

Wednesday is fine, gloriously fine for this more than holiday outing, and if a day off routine is always exhilarating, it is doubly so to be off when others are working. It is why playing truant is so much more satisfactory than official holiday. And today there is also the wonderfully pleasant feeling of having it both ways at once —of playing truant certainly, but also of being virtuously justified in this slipping-off into the hopeful new morning.

I zigzag through the busy central traffic by long-practised side-roads, through the inner suburbs (today all the traffic-lights change to green to greet me), through the houses with gardens, into the Green Belt, and out along country roads. The main traffic is moving into London, not out as I am, and the roads are half-empty—my half is empty. It is a morning of faint haze, pearly with the light of a half-veiled sun not yet high enough in the sky to draw up the mist through the motionless air. I am crossing the hills now, faster and faster, with growing impatience, as if the field might vanish unless I arrive to confirm it.

Planning. *What?*

And now at last the lane up from the village, and as I climb the hill to the field the sun floats clear in a pale blue sky and the valley lies warm and dry in the gentle light.

I am early. I have driven out much too fast. But the bull-dozer is already here, an enormous steel presence on the road-side grass by the gate to the field. There is nothing else but the machine, no driver, no oil cans, only this motionless metal crea-ture like a dumb obedient animal arrived by itself for the day's work ahead. Its tracks are still sticky with yellowish mud—clay I suppose—an alien soil in this dry chalk valley.

I am joined by the next-door dog. It is friendly but not demonstrative (a mutual attitude) and stands beside me looking at the bull-dozer. I consider the machine with a satisfaction as solid as itself, much reassured by its huge size and obvious power. I would climb up and sit experimentally in the driver's seat cantilevered out so invitingly on its single steel arm, but I can hear a car coming along the lane and it is likely to be the crea-ture's keeper. When the car is still the length of the field away it begins to slow up and comes gently to rest beside me. It is in cities that cars stop with a lurch of brakes; in the country they simply cease to move from lack of propulsion. I suddenly realize that the London I left little more than an hour ago is at an immeasurable distance of time and place.

The car door opens slowly and a large peaceful man climbs out. He is quite astonishingly like his bull-dozer. Not the mud, for his coat is as clean as his gleaming new motor-car, but he has the same air of slow power, the same suggestion of awkward but accurate movement. And I suppose a bull-dozer can transform its driver to its own likeness just as much as the proverbial horse or dog, or perhaps it is only that like seeks out like from the start, but certainly this driver and machine are two halves of a single homogeneous whole.

We approach to greet each other, shake hands firmly, intro-duce ourselves, and exchange remarks about the weather—That

it's the ideal day for the job—That it looks like settled fair—
That we're very fortunate—the statements and agreements with
pauses between which are the countryman's way of marking
time while he sizes up a new acquaintance.

Along the lane there is the noise of an approaching tractor,
and my companion is suddenly concerned for his immaculate
car. He climbs back in unexpectedly nimbly and drives it on to
the rough grass verge to leave the road clear for the tractor to
pass. Then he climbs slowly out again, and from the boot un-
packs various tins and bottles and a water-proof cover. He is
very tidy and methodical as big men often are.

"The lorry'll be along any time now," he says, "with the oil
and water. Meanwhile you'd best show me exactly what you
want done."

We walk to the gate and he stops still in the opening to
consider the prospect suddenly revealed beneath us.

"Nice view you've got," he says with satisfaction. He is not
the man to enthuse as I do, but he studies it slowly from east to
west as if he were unrolling a Chinese scroll, and finally nods his
approval. "Very nice *indeed*."

He lifts the gate open and we walk down the sunny field to
the four cricket-stumps, which suddenly look very rakish under
his careful scrutiny. He considers me sideways and smiles.

"Yes," I admit, "I daresay they're not quite true" (more than
that I will not allow). "But that's the size of the house, and that's
where we want it." And what we would like him to do, I explain, is level a terrace for the house, with space for paths all
round it, and cut out a drive up to the road, where he'll need to
make a gap in the hedge for the entrance, and fill in the ditch
with any chalk left over.

"Fine," he says, looking backwards and forwards along the
hill-side in quick calculation. "Fine. But the drive'll be a steepish
climb. The field's got more of a slope than it looks."

I know about the slope, but that is his concern I feel, not

mine. What I must look after is the garden I hope to make when
the house is built. For even I have seen enough new sites, and
read enough gardening books, to know what happens if builders
and bull-dozers are left to themselves. (It is why I am here,
though I would not tell him so.) They dig and level with no
thought at all of anything growing on the desolate area they
leave when they finish. They bury the untidy top-soil and weeds
—the *precious* top-soil which matters more than all else in a
garden. They spread it with layers of sub-soil, covering it irretrievably with inches and feet of crude unweathered clay or
sand or chalk.

I consider how I can make my next pronouncement sufficiently serious, for clearly the driver is not the kind of man one
can keep on reminding when once he starts working. What I
want him to do, I explain in a clear and careful voice, is to strip
off every scrap of grass and top-soil, and even the best of the sub-
soil, before he begins leveling, and keep it all carefully aside to
spread on top again when he has finished. I elaborate—about
burying nothing but chalk, and so on—hoping to make it more
emphatic.

"Alright," he smiles. "I can see you're a gardener and I've
met you gardeners before. You're Tartars, that's what. Watch
like a cat with a mouse to be sure I don't lose the least scoop of
dirt." (He is clearly no gardener himself, for no gardener would
ever describe his precious soil as dirt.) "Alright," he says, "I
know all about it. But you won't find there's much soil to save
on this slope of hill. I'll be down to the chalk pretty well right
away. You'll see when I start."

He walks back to the gate followed by the dog, takes off his
tidy coat, folds it deliberately inside-out and puts it neatly in the
hedge-bottom with the water-can and tarpaulin and his can of
lunch. He climbs into a suit of overalls smudged with different
soils like an artist's smock with paint, then he turns to greet his
machine. It is exactly that: as if the bull-dozer were a friendly

old horse which he feeds and harnesses and generally prepares for work. And all the time he has a comfortable air of being as familiar with this huge creature as I am with the old motor-car I have driven for so many years that I am no longer conscious of driving it, but simply sit inside and it moves about of its own accord.

To me the bull-dozer seems an enormous monster, with its seat at head-level and its gleaming steel scoop six feet across. But it's not their largest, the driver says with a fatherly air. He un-screws taps and pushes various levers in and out. Then he seeks out a suitably enormous hammer from the tool-box and hits his machine's steel flanks here and there in a friendly way as if he were patting a horse.

"We've another one nearly twice this size," he goes on. "But I reckon this one's big enough for this little job."

While the dog and I watch him the lorry arrives with cans of oil and water. The lorry-driver admires the view in his turn (it is what everyone does as soon as they arrive I notice), then they unload the cans together and feed the machine with the liquid calories it needs for the work ahead. The driver now moves with increasing purpose. There is more wrenching and hammer-patting, which I suppose with a horse would be checking the harness. Then the moment has come. He starts up the engine.

I had expected a certain amount of noise, but I am utterly unprepared for the stupefying roar which now fills the whole echoing valley and sends the birds flying up in alarm from all the trees along the hedges. The din is so violent that it is like a physical assault, and I retreat in dismay to the slight shelter of a car with closed windows. The dog has gone already, hurrying off through the gap in the hedge at twice the pace he has ever moved before. One thing is certain—once started there can be no more instructions about what we want, and I only hope the driver has understood.

He is up on the seat now, edging his huge machine in

through the gate, tilting at an alarming angle as he drops down from the level of the road, and with only an inch or two to spare on either side between the gate-posts. I am reassured to see that he manœuvres his monster as neatly as he folds his coat. His skill is exact and accurate, and as soon as I am acclimatized to the noise, I sit in the hedge-bottom and watch fascinated as he strips an area of field ready for leveling. It is exactly like watching a surgeon perform a giant operation. First he skims off the grass as neatly as turning back a scalp, then he scrapes away the thin flesh of soil to expose the bare white bones of the chalk beneath.

It is strange for the ground to be white like this. We think of the earth beneath us as dark and blind, but this chalk is a dazzling white far brighter than anything else in the landscape. Will the driver call this dirt I wonder? But he is right about the soil, there is no more than two or three inches under the grass to pile up in the mounds he is saving as I asked.

It is always a pleasure to watch skilled workers engrossed in what they are doing, and this driver is so expertly skilled that he and his machine are a single unit, a steel-fleshed working creature with a man for its controlling brain. It is exactly like watching an animal of an unknown species, a kind of earth-moving dragon.

For the next hour the roaring and manœuvring go on without a break in a rising and falling sea of sound, and the area of flayed field grows steadily larger until the rectangle of exposed white chalk is twice the size of the grass enclosed by my cricket-stumps. Then the machine halts sideways on the slope, the engine sinks to a low rumble, then dies completely, and at once a wonderful relief of silence floods back into the valley.

The driver climbs down from his seat which is like a canti-levered spoon, surveys his work from ground-level, then joins me in the hedge-bottom. He looks disapprovingly at me sitting on the ground, shocked as country people always are, that any-one should sit unconcerned on the treacherous grass. Asking for your death, they say, and You'll suffer with the rheumatics later on I'll be bound. And even when the ground is baked hard with drought and heat, they still feel that the scarcely surviving grass is somehow a deadly peril.

The driver unfolds his tarpaulin and spreads it out carefully over the carpet of dry leaves which has been my comfortable seat all morning. I watch him hesitate whether to offer me part of his cover, but he decides not, and settles down himself.

"Is that what you want?" He nods at the raw white gash across the green meadow.

"Yes. That's exactly it. Thank you for saving the grass and soil so carefully."

"Had no choice, did I? I realized it was as much as my job's worth to bury so much as a blade of grass with you looking on." And he smiles at me with complete equanimity, clearly quite unconcerned about any fuss I might make but amiably willing to humour me.

"I can see this isn't the first plot you've levelled," I tell him.

"No, that it's not. Not by some hundreds of acres. Spent the whole war levelling runways for the R.A.F. Not on good clear ground like this neither. Jungles it was mostly. Mind if I smoke?"

He lights his pipe and we sit companionably under the hedge considering the valley in front of us. The pale lemon sun shines from a pale azure sky with an effect not so much of sunlight as of irradiated air. Through the faint silvery haze the landscape is delicate and remote like a landscape in a dream, an insubstantial vision which could vanish like a rainbow. I wonder what the driver is thinking about, but we sit and say nothing, savouring the unaccustomed quiet—a pleasure as vivid and positive after the morning's din as a long drink when thirsty. And as my ears recover from the bombardment of noise, I begin to hear again the faint sounds which make up the background of quiet, a dog barking far-off on the other hill-side, the pink, pink of a chaffinch in the hedge behind us, and from the farm at the top of the valley a distant thin whine of sawing-up logs for the winter.

Suddenly I remember the coffee I brought from London and go to fetch it from the car. I have brought an extra mug but forgotten sugar for the driver. As we sip it we go on looking at the valley over the rim of our mugs through the rising steam. It is wonderfully peaceful.

"Very nice," says the driver to thank me for the coffee. "Very nice indeed." But I think he is only being polite because of the sugar. He takes my empty mug and rinses them both with water from his can, then he wipes them carefully with a twist of dry grass before he hands them back, and I think how good he must be in the house. He sits down again on his tarpaulin and we go on studying the view.

"The thing about the chalk," he says, "is it's never sticky. No matter if it's been raining for a week on end and stopped no more than an hour ago, it's still never sticky. Drains through as fast as it falls. Never sticky."

It is evident that this obliging drainage of the chalk is one of his life's satisfactions. And so it will be for me, I think contentedly, in the gardening years ahead.

"But this levelling now," he goes on. "Do you just want it straight like I've cleared the grass off—with a drop at the front and a bank at the back?"

By the tone of his voice I realize that it is not in the least what this earth-shaper would want for his own house.

"Well, I think it must be straight along the front," but I am hesitant now, for I have realized that a bull-dozer offers all kinds of new possibilities for adapting the site. But on the other hand the house is already designed.

"There's to be a retaining wall at the front," I tell him. "And a terrace for sitting out all along the south of the house."

"I see." He accepts this without comment. "But what about the back? Wouldn't you like a nice, easy sweep like, to the bank

· 119 ·

behind? I can cut it back a bit if you'd fancy—opposite where you come out the door. Make the bank a bit steep though," he adds consideringly. "It's a pretty fair slope. More than it looks. I can feel it in my machine."

But what do I care about the steepness of banks? Here is power and creation. A mound here, I can say, a hollow there, and the drive to sweep round in a long banked curve climbing up the slope. I am only glad the boys are not here as well, or there would certainly be no escaping a swimming-pool. For here is a tool which transforms mere man to a force of nature, a twentieth-century machine more wondrous by far than Saint Cecilia's.

While the driver has lunch, I decide, I shall go down to the village for a bundle of bamboo canes to work out the plan. Then while he starts levelling the terrace at the far end, which is simple, I shall try to work out the curves of the bank and the drive at the other end. Then he can come and see if I have got it right before he starts digging.

So all afternoon I mark out curves with rows of bamboos, alter them, alter them again, then pull them all out and start afresh. For quite apart from any expert interest in graceful curves, it is far more difficult than anyone would suppose to loop a drive up a varying slope and keep the climb even all the way.

As for the terrace where the bull-dozer is working, that is now a major operation on the poor unresisting field, cutting down through broken chalk to the solid white rock of the hill beneath. And as the machine moves steadily backwards and forwards all afternoon, the long level platform for the house grows steadily wider, with the chalk scooped out from the bank at the back pushed over the steadily increasing cliff at the front.

The chalk to look at is exactly uniform, of a white so dazzling that even in this pale winter sunshine we keep our eyes half-closed against the glare. But the rock must be harder in some places than others, for from time to time the engine whines with the effort of scooping it out, hesitates, then goes on again with a deeper roar, crumbling the rock into piles of white rubble quite astonishingly larger than the space they came from.

The afternoon is peaceful in its noisy fashion. The bull-dozer continues its purposeful slow crawling, I push in rows of bamboos then take them out again, and the sun slides down the sky towards the western hills. Now and again the driver halts his machine, climbs down to pick up something I can't see, and examines it carefully. He has stopped thus mysteriously several times during the day, but this time he comes over to show me what he has found.

"It's a bit of an exploded meteorite," he says, showing me a shapeless scrap of what might be rusty metal.

"Is it?" I say with interest, for certainly it is an interesting theory.

"Yes. That's what they tell me," he says. "I like to keep a sharp look-out. You can't never tell what you're liable to find when once you start digging. And anything I come on I take along to the museum to see. All manner of things—fossils, Roman remains, everything. And they're always ready to tell you. The museum it was that told me about the meteorite, or I'd never of known."

Once he was levelling a field for a farmer down in the Vale, he goes on. At Princes Risborough. And he came on the foundations of the Black Prince's palace. "Coloured tiles," he says. "All manner of bits. I took some along and they told me. But there's never anything much to be found on these hills. There's no history here," so he sadly pronounces. For he is not in the least impressed, as I contantly am, to find everywhere bits of broken pots buried deep under the grass. "You'll always find broken pots," he says indifferently. "No matter where you dig." And I remember an archaeologist friend once telling me that when with prodigious effort they raised one of the stones at

Stonehenge, they found underneath it a Keiller's marmalade jar. (Or was it a bottle of port and a welcoming letter? And was it Avebury not Stonehenge? My details are unreliable always. But anyway a find as disillusioning for them as the broken pots for the driver.) For odd bits of plates and mugs are not what he means by history. That has to be something far more important than simply the astonishing wealth of past life over every mile of English soil, layer on forgotten layer. History means something he can take to the museum one day and be told he has made an important find. And the best of all are Roman remains, for to him the Romans seem prehistoric half-mythical beings, who came to this commonplace country from some strange magical land across the seas. It does not count that the huge earth ramparts crowning the hill behind us were there before the Romans even set out from Rome. "Yes. Very interesting." But earth, so his tone implies, is still only earth (only dirt, I suppose), even if it was piled up some little time ago. Whereas Roman remains are a very different matter, and anything Roman can count as buried treasure.

So I help him to look for history in return for the soil he saves so carefully. Clearly he regards it as a mild form of madness to hoard every grain of soil as if it were gold-dust, but nonetheless he treats it with a kindly tolerance, cheerfully allowing for an enthusiasm as watchful as his own. And since enthusiasts are ridiculous in exact proportion to our indifference to their enthusiasm, and since I care more for his history-hunting than he does for my soil-saving, he therefore seems less absurd to me than I do to him, and his tolerance is therefore a greater virtue than mine.

But, alas, all I find him in return for my heaps of soil is a George V half-penny, green with the mildew of buried years. And since that clearly can't count as history I shall keep it myself, and set it like a plaque in the concrete of the doorway to commemorate this first happy stage of our house-building.

Planning. *What?*

The first day the terrace—a smooth white platform edged into the hill-side like a tray waiting for a house to be set on it. The second day the entrance. I felt only the faintest twinge of remorse when the bull-dozer pared off the grassy skin of the unoffending field, but the entrance is different. The entrance is horrible. For we must make a gap through our beautiful hedge, a gap about twenty feet wide, so it seems, for the drive will slant through at an angle to the road, and will have to be well banked-up on the field side because of the slope. So twenty feet or more of hedge will have to be cleared out, so the driver says.

I am horrified. Of course I knew we should have to make some sort of way in, since the farm gate is at the wrong end of the field for the house. But I only imagined one or two haw-thorn bushes cut down for a narrow entrance without disturb-ing any of the precious trees. And now a whole twenty-foot length must be sacrificed.

However carefully I choose the strip of hedge such a huge gash will take several trees with it. And trees are not like grass, an anonymous green skin which renews itself by spreading back over wounds. Trees are separate individuals. When we destroy one we kill a creature, an unconscious vegetable creature no doubt, but still a separate entity with its own self-contained life.

But destroy them we must. It is only a question of which shall go, for although the entrance is more or less fixed by the position of the house, there is still some latitude in either direc-tion. I can choose which trees to offer as vegetable sacrifice to the gods who preside over the building of houses.

Certainly not either of the beeches whose twigs are a purple-brown haze in the winter sun. Nor the young ash with its ferny pattern of leaves against last summer's sky. Nor the old larch overgrown with ivy where the stock-doves nested, nor the crab-apple which was a mound of pink and white all last spring. And I must save the biggest of the spindle-trees, and the wayfaring-tree which has grown up through the hedge and is swagged in August with waxy bunches of traveller's joy (if we chose by names what a suitable marriage). There is really nothing expendable. Could we tunnel a way in perhaps, as eighteenth-century mansions tunnelled a way to the kitchen, to pretend they had souls above food?

"It's no good," the driver interrupts firmly. "I can see you don't like it, but you'll just have to make up your mind and let me get on." He is a kindly doctor reasoning with a nervous patient. "Unless I clear out a fair stretch of hedge you'll never get in and out at all. What's so special about this bit anyway? Looks much like any other hedge to me. Needs laying of course."

The whole hedge is special. Needs laying indeed! But he is a practical countryman and I am only an impractical Londoner, and anyway something must go.

Would it do if he took out those hawthorns and hedge-maples between the beech and the wayfaring-tree?

"No, it wouldn't. Not half wide enough."

Oh dear. Then the wayfaring-tree and the next yard or two of nothing in particular?

"Might be enough, but I doubt it. I'd think that holly would have to go and that next big bush." (The bush is another hedge-maple.)

Well, will he start just clear of the beech-tree and destroy as little as possible?

He starts. It is dreadful. He wedges one point of his scoop into the base of the unsuspecting victim, puts the engine in bottom gear, and pushes. The tree shudders, the engine whines, there is a horrible cracking noise like teeth being broken from a jaw, and the assaulted tree lies murdered in the ditch.

Planning. *What?*

The driver climbs down and comes over to where I watch in misery.

"I should go away and do something else if I were you. I've got to get on and you're not going to like it."

This is how doctors, no doubt, advise the parents of children they operate on. Does William? I wonder. But parents would never be let near enough to his operating theatre to make themselves a nuisance to him, as I clearly am to the driver. And he is kind and patient—"I'll not take out a single twig more than I must. You don't have to worry."

So dismissed, I have really no choice. I go down to the village and stay away firmly an hour by my watch. And when I come back the gap is horrible, a huge jagged wound bleeding with white ends of torn-off roots like severed blood-vessels. And the field is littered with fallen trees like the victims of some dreadful massacre, broken bodies savagely murdered and callously left unburied.

But even as I shudder at the violence, I also register with detached interest what an astonishing amount of vegetation has come from a single hole. Wide as the gap is, it still seems impossible that it contained all this, piles of branches and twigs and general hedge tangle, and the trunks of what I thought were only overgrown shrubs, but lying on the field look like forest trees. It is mass murder, nothing less. And the hedge-bottom where they were wrenched from is torn and pulpy like bleeding gums.

"Don't you worry. We'll soon get it cleared up and ship-shape. Now its once over you'll never notice. And I'll pile all the trash up together. You've only to leave it to dry out and you'll have a fine blaze next spring."

He is a long-suffering doctor and I am a patient with the vapours. And certainly by evening the wound is much less offensive. He has levelled the loose soil in the hedge-bottom, and the weight of the bull-dozer has firmed it to a solid surface. He has cleared up the corpses as he promised, and from so much rough mechanical handling the vegetable victims have lost all identity and are now no more than so much bonfire material. I am resigned now even if not reconciled, and when on the third day he cuts out the drive in a long graceful loop sweeping up the slope and out to the road, the gap in the hedge becomes a positive achievement.

The three-day interlude is nearly over, three days of a curious dream-like remoteness despite the noise. Indeed it is partly the noise itself which has isolated them, the constant roar like a barrier between our life in the field and the outside world, like living behind a waterfall of sound. The weather too has been curiously other-worldly, like days in a dream: the air completely still, with unseen larks trilling deliriously in the empty sky, and the country round us like a water-colour painting in delicate greens and browns and misty blues.

The driver is finishing-off. "I like to leave a job tidy," he says. "Never like to leave a mess behind me for someone else to clear." He sets his scoop at an oblique angle and smooths off the bank behind the house, making sure it curves round into the edge of the drive to his critical satisfaction. He collects up the last odd heaps of chalk and piles them against the ramp, which now carries the drive over the ditch beyond the hedge. He smooths and tidies and finishes-off like a housewife clearing up after the builders, using his six-foot scoop as exactly and delicately as a six-inch shovel. At last the field is tidy again, even by his fastidious standards, and he comes over to consult me.

"Is there anything else you want done before I go? Now's the time to say. I'm not in no hurry for half-an-hour, so anything else you can think of."

But the things I want done need a great deal longer than half-an-hour. I have all kinds of plans, but this is no time to produce them. Except—Yes—Would he peel off the grass from a patch of ground up by the hedge? (I show him where.) Then when it's rotted down I can spread it back over the chalk and use it as a nursery bed.

"Right-o. And while I do it, you think if there's anything else. No point in doing jobs by hand you know, when I'm here to save you labour."

But I can think of nothing, or rather nothing small enough, and we take a last walk round the site to admire his meticulous operations. We walk up the drive which seems most alarmingly steep now it is a bare road-like surface and not indeterminate hill-side camouflaged by rough grass.

"It climbs *steady* enough," he says consideringly. "But it's pretty steep. All right for my machine of course, but I wouldn't be too sure about cars in winter. I wouldn't wonder if you didn't have to get me back here again, to cut a wider sweep and level it out a bit."

But what do I care about the drive? A mere skimming-off of grass and a scrape of soil to expose the solid chalk surface. We will see how the builders' lorries manage, I tell him (and I can plan out the garden, I tell myself, ambitious now with glorious schemes for moving earth and altering levels). For I will certainly have the bull-dozer back, I decide, and a new drive will be an excellently sensible excuse. Or why not have it for a Christmas present? A day for Christmas and a day for my birthday?

The machine is up by the road-side now, driven out through our fine new entrance. The driver has taken off his chalky over-alls and folds them away in the boot of his car. It is rather sad.

"Well. I'd better be off. Else I'll be in trouble with the wife for keeping the tea waiting. They'll fetch the machine away first thing tomorrow I shouldn't wonder. Anyway won't hurt where it is for a day or two. A bit heavy for anyone to make off with I reckon."

We shake hands and he climbs into the car. He starts the engine but still makes no move to go, only sitting there peacefully as if he had all the time in the world despite his tea-keeping wife. He winds down the window and I thank him again for doing so exactly what we wanted.

"I like to leave a good job," he says. "And anyway it's

straightforward enough with a clear space to work in. It's when there's scarce room to turn that it's tricky. Enjoyed it too, I must say. Quite a holiday it's been working up here." He looks round the evening landscape and a wood-owl hoots hollowly on the hill above us. "Well. I reckon I'd better be off," he says, making resolute motions at last with gears and handbrake, and carefully bouncing his car off the grass verge and on to the road. He leans out of the window to shake hands a second time.

"I'll be seeing you again I shouldn't wonder," and he grins at me as if he knew he was reading my thoughts. "I can't see you being satisfied with that little bit now you've once got the hang of it."

⟡⟡⟡⟡ 19 ⟡⟡⟡⟡

The human mind is essentially self-centred. It is not an instrument for the impartial registering of outside reality, but for receiving the specialized information about reality which is sent in by our animal senses, and for creating from that very limited evidence a particular version of the world as it concerns our specialized human existence.

We have no way of perceiving abstract reality. Why should we have, since it does not concern us? Our concern, like any other animal's, is to perceive the world around us in such a way that we are able to survive in it. What we accept as valid reality is only our limited human-survival version of the immensely complicated and mostly unknown world outside ourselves.

If the human mind had developed as an impartial recorder of facts, then human creatures could never have survived in so perilous a setting as the eat-or-be-eaten world we live in. We should none of us be here if our ape-ancestors had sat about registering a tree as a tree, instead of as a source of food and a retreat from enemies. We are like the blind man who perceives a bus as a step and a handrail and nothing else. It is all that concerns him directly and all he can understand. The world we experience is not reality but our own creation. Our limited human consciousness selects from the unlimited inhuman facts only those which concern our particular state, and from them creates a version of the universe which is relevant for our way of living.

It is why science is so alien to the non-scientific mind. For science is concerned with understanding the world with as little human distortion as possible. Its aim is to create a version of abstract reality, not in terms of our animal and emotional life, but as impartial fact existing separately from human beings. It is why the findings of science are so indigestible for the human consciousness. Even a century and a half ago our indigestion worried Shelley: today it would probably seem to him a mortal sickness.

The slope of the field is steeper than I thought it was. That is all I set out to say. It is *much* steeper. Yet I can walk up and down it easily and it should therefore be more or less flat. For in our every-man-his-own-creation version of any scene, our own experience is for us the ultimate truth. And since we are each the measure of our own universe, we have only to stand upright to know the absolute vertical by which the outside world can be judged. We stand vertical: the ground we stand on must therefore be horizontal. But this field I stand on is not horizontal. Judged by the terrace as level, it is steep. Most surprisingly steep.

There are times of course when the surface beneath us quite clearly does not conform to the logical level state. We can *feel* (by the discomfort in our feet, by the pressure of our toes against our shoes) that the ground is off-true with our own infallible upright. But since our senses are only concerned with what affects our human living, we only judge slopes by the very rough measure of how they affect our movement. We are not concerned with surveying but only with walking up-hill. It is why whese lanes are so much steeper on a bicycle than on foot, cyclists being more sensitive to slopes than walkers.

This slope is easy to walk up. Therefore it is not steep. Certainly the spirit-level reported otherwise, but that was an abstract fact not confirmed by my senses, and until now I have had no way of experiencing for myself the spirit-level's findings. For the chalk hills are not steep to look at. Their rounded slopes merge into each other so smoothly and gently that they give no consciousness of sharp gradients. In this landscape of flowing hills with no horizontals to judge by, there has been nothing to disturb my comfortable sense of the field sloping shallowly down to the valley floor.

But now there is. The terrace is horizontal, and the terrace wedges into the hill at a quite ridiculous tipped-up angle. Clearly something is wrong.

Had he left it higher at the front, I asked the driver before he left, to allow for the chalk to settle during the winter? "No," he said. "It's pretty well level as it is. You won't find this chalk'll settle much. It makes a good firm bed from the start. I can tell it's level by the feel of my machine. It's the lie of the land you're going by. Very deceptive. Very. I reckon you'll find the level's near enough true when you come to measure it up."

But mere assurance of fact does not convince our senses. For me the terrace is only level because I have hung a stone on a string from a bamboo cane like a fish on a fishing-rod pushed into the ground, and seen that the fall is exactly at right-angles to the surface of the terrace. And even I am enough of a scientist to believe that gravity is more reliable than my personal judgment.

However, it is still no more than an intellectual conviction, and if I am to *feel* that the terrace is level I must concentrate on that single fact and readjust the landscape until it conforms. But it is not easy. I suppose until now my mind has compromised by sharing out the angle of the slope between terrace and hill-side, tilting each of them equally, so that field and terrace meet in a shallow V-shape with both arms equally inclined to the horizontal. But every time I look at it I am disconcerted to imagine a house built at such an odd tipping angle. It is like sitting on the deck of a rolling ship and seeing what should be the level horizon slope alarmingly across the sky like a watery hill-side.

I sit and look at the terrace, mentally wrenching it to a right-angle with the uncompromising vertical of the hanging string, and levering up the hill behind in compensation. The slope of the hill-side steepens while I watch. But it is a strenuous exercise in visual-mental adjustment, and I have only to look away for a moment for the hill to settle back to its former level, tilting up the terrace again as it sinks. Until the house is there to hold it down, the terrace will never be firmly fixed, but will sway like the light end of a seesaw whenever I let go.

However, I am adjusted enough now to accept that the slope is far steeper than I believed, *visually* steeper, for in terms of human movement it is only slightly off-level. We can walk up and down it unconcerned, there is no sense of falling away down-hill.

But the terrace has tilted back. I shall knock the four cricket-stumps in again and set them vertical. Perhaps they will peg it down. I measure out the now familiar plan and hammer them in at the corners with a stone. The enclosed rectangle looks very small on the white expanse of its tray. Will that tiny area really hold all the rooms we intend? Is it big enough to house a family? I collect a bundle of branches from the bonfire heap and divide the house-space into rooms marked out by wavering dark lines of twigs. I gather flints turned up in the chalk and set them as the edges of the window-frames.

And suddenly I have built the house, solid and square. I have projected reality. So children must feel when they build brick outlines of houses, or make rows of pebbles and lines on the sand which are towers and unscaleable ramparts. Not pebbles as mere make-shift for a tower, but a tower indeed, with gaunt grey walls and turreted sky-line, and the pebbles no more than the convenient evocative symbol of the solid reality. The tower is real, not the pebbles; so this house is real, not the twigs and stones which are mere indications of reality to an incomplete world of uninterested beings lacking one of the necessary senses to perceive it.

Between these four stumps on the hill-side there is an exact enclosure in space. It is no longer a small indeterminate amount of the volume of air in the valley, but a definite place with a separate identity.

Just here, by the window-stones of this particular twig-enclosure which is the kitchen, we shall sit round the table hundreds of times eating hundreds of meals. Suspended in this exact point in space we shall lie in bed, here lie in the bath, here sit at night in a room which is a bright warm box set exactly and rigidly at this point in space in the enormous night of encircling darkness. It is this exact perspective of the hills across the valley which will become as familiar to us as the shape of our own faces, which we shall live with until we die, and our children perhaps after us.

And indeed this phantom house is haunted by ghosts of the future as other houses are haunted by the past: by the hundreds of human beings who will so intensively occupy this tiny space of air in the empty countryside. Unborn people who will laugh and sing and quarrel and weep, women who will dream futures for the children they are pregnant with, men who will make difficult decisions about their lives. Children will grow up here and remember it always with the inexplicable significance of early experience. And it is strange to think that by piling a few bricks together we dictate a place where people will be born and will die, that we fix for unknown strangers the exact setting for their sudden radiant moments of happiness and their long days of unshakable despair.

There are times when I feel that to build a house which other people must live in is a quite unwarrantable interference with their privacy, as if we invaded their most intimate lives and insisted how they must arrange them.

On this blank terrace, in this motionless winter air, I am almost palpably haunted by our future ghosts, but invisible presences, for I cannot even imagine what they might look like. They are there. If I turned quickly I should face them. But I still should not see them: it is only their nearness I am conscious of in the ambiguous light of this indefinable suspended season of the year. And later on even their presence will vanish, for it is one of the things always strange to me in any house—that the people who live in it at any moment dominate it completely. No matter how intense the lives of those who were there before us, they leave no consciousness, but vanish with no more trace than last year's snows. Simply by changing the tenants of a house all the other lives within it are destroyed. A new wall-paper, different furniture, and a whole way of living is gone: the present inhabitants are the only inhabitants always.

Yet for each of us our own experience of living is the one overwhelming reality. So intense is our personal awareness of the world that we do not even feel how minute a part it is of the general human consciousness. For it is not only our general conception of reality which is unique to our human species, but each individual's conception is also unique to the mind which conceives it. The world we each experience as real does not exist apart from our individual selves. It is our own personal creation, a particular synthesis from the observable facts by the action of a particular personality. And since each human being is different from every other, so is their impression of the world they live in.

There are as many versions of reality as there are individuals to observe it, and we each of us inhabit a unique universe.

When we die, the world as we know it dies with us. If I killed myself now as I sit here with the valley in front of me, I should destroy not only myself but the view I am looking at. The valley would still be there for others to see, but not the particular version of it which exists in my consciousness. For others can no more see my view of the valley than I can see theirs. My eyes record it differently, my mind interprets it by its own particular values, and the associations it rouses belong to my own individual life which is different from everyone else's who has ever lived. And we have no way of sharing the particular consciousness of the world which for each of us is our only experience of the human state. When any of us is obliterated an irreplaceable human version of the world is obliterated with us. We and our world die together.

Even this house will survive us: a few bricks piled together at our bidding. For we shall vanish. But fortunately so will the ghosts of the future who today disturb me. For when the house is built and we live inside it, our solid occupation will crowd out their phantom presences. They will not be uninvited guests at our table, nor wandering souls in the night. They will not share our warm rooms as invisible companions. For once moved in we shall occupy the house as completely as noise occupies silence, and as solidly as the chairs and cupboards. The ghosts will have gone like forgotten dreams, for it is only this unoccupied shadow of a house which harbours such shadows.

Planning. *What?*

◇◇◇◇◇ *20* ◇◇◇◇◇

It is a year since we started, since the first vague uneasiness which was the first sign of the coming upheaval. Only a year, a single small pad of twelve paper months on the calendar, and my old red diary changed for a new green one. But last year is a lifetime away, and it is not a different year that my diary records but a different existence. For a year I have waked and slept and moved and talked and thought and dreamed—house. Nothing else has penetrated to any permanent level of awareness. That most of the actual time of this last year has been spent in London still does not mean I have lived there, for our life is not what happens to us but what we are conscious of happening. It is why outside events are so unhelpful a guide in understanding another person. And what I have been conscious of for the past year is an unbuilt house: a structure at first floating uneasily above the Buckinghamshire hills, then brought down firmly to earth on exact foundations. An unbuilt house and all the rest mere interruption.

But now, praise be, there is a lull. The builders will start in the spring, they say, but it is now undeniably winter. There is nothing to do but wait. The spring will come no sooner for my insistence, nor later for my indifference. I can be peaceful and recover. For the year has been exhausting, and now I can cut off my driving impatience and settle back on the slowly revolving seasons.

Besides, I am bored with the whole affair. I am sick and tired of house-making. We will build a new house. Yes. But thousands of houses are built every year without all this emotional pother. Surely reasonable people can have a few bricks built up and a roof put on top without pouring out a year of their lives to do it. Probably they can, but I am not reasonable people, it seems, and I cannot.

Nonetheless I am bored. With the boredom which follows preoccupation as depression follows elation. For when we come back after any break in our usual life there is always this period of restless emptiness before our local values grow again to importance. It is like the sudden empty silence which followed the bull-dozer's roar when the engine stopped. But gradually in that newly established quiet the indigenous noises of the valley returned to the surface and became significant again in the re-woven web of country sounds, and now that the din of my preoccupation has also died down I am conscious again of the normal affairs of London living. For the next few months the house can be left in some safe oblivion and I shall forget it. After all it is only an interlude; there is still the solidly established rhythm of living which it interrupted. If it were not for my unbalanced single-mindedness it need not even be a separate interlude, but only an extra line of counterpoint in the general pattern.

Since human affairs need human energy to drive them as engines need fuel, I shall no doubt have to start up again next spring when the house starts building. But meanwhile I can enjoy a peaceful switched-off winter, and recover from obsession. I shall consider the time from now till spring as a cold-weather holiday-at-home with the long-neglected, re-adopted, newly delightful family. And forget the house.

Though not entirely forget it. There are still things to do. They are only not urgent, and can be fitted into a reasonable routine of time and attention. There are bricks to choose for a start. Unless they are ordered soon, so the builders warn us, they won't be delivered in time to start next spring. Very well we shall choose them—it is simple enough. But like everything else about building a house it is not simple at all. To begin with, one single brick, or even half-a-dozen or so in the shelves at the

Planning. *What?*

Building Centre, give not the least idea of what a whole wall of the same bricks would look like. Nor is it any great help to consider indoors by electric light a surface which will stand out under the open sky. And don't forget you must see them both in sun and shade, my brother warned, and both wet and dry. For bricks, so we find, change colour dramatically when they are damp, which in England is much of the time. Nor had I ever realized how subtle are the variations of brickish texture, nor how much it matters what they are made of and how they are moulded. I had never before really *seen* the bricks of buildings except as a vague general impression of plant-pot red, or London yellow, or the thunder-cloud grey of modern architects. But now I have become a brick-fancier, and amass all manner of fascinating new information—that sand-faced bricks have a matt surface—that wire-cutting gives a crumbly look—that hand-made bricks have a special finish like soft leather crumpled. And what I had certainly never noticed before are the endless processions of brick-lorries everywhere on all the roads. Every other lorry now seems loaded with bricks, stacked at a slight angle to slip inwards to the centre and packed with straw between the layers. It is clear proof, if anyone still needed it, that we see only what we are already conscious of, looking with our brains as much as our eyes.

This winter we collect samples of bricks as other people collect paper-weights, and we take them out at week-ends to study in the country setting of the Regency Villa garden. Gradually the patch of lawn outside the kitchen window is covered with little piles of different bricks like a children's nursery floor. We consider them by sun and shadow, in dry weather and wet as we were told to. We study them against green grass and blue sky and a fine assortment of grey and white clouds. For after all, the colour of the bricks is as important for a house as the colour of cloth we choose for a coat. The ones we decide on will not only be the whole outside fabric of the house, but even from inside will frame the view in every window. And as always we must compromise—between bricks we like but which take nine months to deliver, and bricks we like less—between bricks we like and bricks we can afford. For though to a butter-buying housewife a brick seems a fine solid slab to cost as little as sixpence, yet a thousand sixpences for a thousand bricks seems much less of a bargain.

At last we find a sample which will do. Yes, we can have them for spring. Yes, we can afford them. Yes, they are made close enough to the site for transport to be reasonable. And yes, we like them. Alas, that the liking should come at the end of the list. But of course it never does; it is simply that for bricks we disliked we never considered the rest of the list to begin with.

The ones we have found are a rough-surfaced soft golden-buff, mostly used to match Cotswold stone, so the makers tell us. Topped with a roof of sanded tiles we hope we shall more or less blend with the hill-side and disturb the valley as little as any house can. For although our proxy conscience-by-planners has approved our house-building, yet now that I have slowed up enough to consider, there is no doubt at all that the valley would be better without us. Not better without our house in particular, but without any buildings of any kind except the farm at the head of the valley. Besides, no one could remember the bull-dozer's brutal operations on the field and the hedge and still feel complacent. They are raw wounds which reproach me afresh every week-end.

But the week-ends are only interludes now, forgotten in the London week. Even the refurbishing of the Regency Villa is an easy-paced and indifferent routine, and I no longer rush at it every time trying to finish if off all at once. For I am not really a steady worker, and my natural way of climbing a mountain is simply to set off non-stop for the top. Which is no way to reach the tops of mountains but only a state of exhaustion, and if this winter lasts long enough I may learn the lasting habit of a steady pace, which would no doubt be more efficient in the end. Though my run and rest method does well enough for the minor and manageable hills, and is more adaptable than a steady pace since to get more done I need only keep running for a longer time, and cut down the resting.

But the house? I consider it without emotion from this chilly winter distance. Permission has come for our plans, and the builders are finally booked for spring. We are ready to start when the time comes, and meanwhile the house is safe in cold-storage.

A hard winter and snow at Christmas. On Boxing Day we coldly furnish forth the day with baked meats, and drive out to picnic on the terrace which we hope is busy consolidating. We arrive, we sweep down the frozen drive in fine disregard of whether we shall ever get up again, we stop on the edge of the terrace like a shallow cliff, four car-doors all open at once like the double wings of a beetle, four people climb out, appreciate the freezing air, climb promptly in again, and close the four doors quickly behind them.

We will picnic inside the car with the windows tight shut and the heater full on, and who cares about being degenerate?

The view of the valley under snow is romantically lovely, the white hills strange and unfamiliar, and brushed with woods which are purple-dark and mysterious in the ghostly landscape. They fringe the hills like rough fur, like sea-weed round the edge of rock-pools. And the snow shines. Is it that the surface has thawed and frozen again to a thin crust of ice which reflects the sun in this pale orange glow? Perhaps. But to find out would mean leaving the boxed-in warmth of the car, and we are none of us Francis Bacon to experiment with cold on freezing hill-sides. In the faint December sunlight the fields are coldly radi-ant, and the swelling curves of the opposite slope are translucent as pearls.

So much I can see from the comfort inside the window. But

it is no good thinking I can admire the view (*our* view now, and there will be plenty more snowy winters) for any longer than it takes to eat cold turkey and slices of Christmas cake. We came to picnic. We have picnicked. Now we will go back again. The family's reasoning is irrefutable.

Wouldn't they like a walk through the woods? I ask hopefully.

No, they wouldn't. They'd like to go back. Today even William is car-bound.

I wind down my window a tentative inch, and the freezing air is an invisible blade of cold. Outside on the edge of the terrace the lumps of broken chalk are encased in ice like jellied eels. Even I am convinced, and back we go to the warmth of London, rushing up the steep and snowy drive in bottom gear with a roar of triumph.

Piles of bricks and ice-bound picnics. Pleasant enough in their way, but skimpy fuel to stoke the fire of enthusiasm in so inexpansive a season. Enthusiasm sinks like a failing flame. Somewhere between January and February it dies completely. Fools build houses for wise men to live in. Were they right after all? The sheep or the goats, whichever they were. Should we give up the whole thing now before it is irretrievably too late?

But I have not reached forty-one (I have winter birthdays) without learning to allow for my alternating elations and despairs. If people were boats I should need extra ballast not extra sail, and I try to provide the ballast by taking thought. For no one can be wholly sane, since sanity is not an absolute state but only an accepted average of mankind in general, and no one is ever exactly average, but only a varying approximation to normal. Depending on our different personalities we each of us vary in different ways, and if the variation widens to abnormality it is the same inherent direction.

For each of us therefore there is a particular form of madness which is our own potential deviation from normal, and mine is manic depression.

Planning. *What?*

"In disturbances of the manic-depressive type, a single mood, either of pleasure or displeasure, persists, and all thoughts and actions in keeping with it are given free rein. Mania and depression are two sides of the same penny and the patient's mood alternates between them."

In my mild, only slightly-off-average way I too swing between alternating moods of depression and elation. I travel through life, not on a level course like walking, but rising and falling like a woodpecker's wavy flight. I suppose it is why I work by my run and rest method, and why I try to reach any height I aim at in a single exhilarating leap and not by steady climbing.

But I know it is inefficient. I know that the tortoise wins, and I try to be a tortoise. I try to divide the impossible whole into possible separate parts and to take them in emotional blinkers one at a time, not in a single extended effort. But dull, dull. I have no interest in the parts unless I can see the whole. Yet I recognize my madness and I try. It is why I make plans in wintry weather before spring sends my spirits soaring. But it is mostly no more than a façade of caution, for I mostly set out in my manic moods and then drown in the following depressions.

It is where I am now, the sinking after the soaring. For my gloom is nothing to do with outside events: there is nothing to dismay me. But we live in a state of siege against sorrow, and when our defences are down, despair is a sickness to which we are dangerously vulnerable.

Nor are our depressions any less real because they have no definable outside reason. They may even be made more tolerable by some definite trouble which concentrates them in a rational cause, as an inch of rain is more tolerable as a thunderstorm than as a week of grey drizzle.

As for the folly of building houses, mid-winter is no time to consider unpalatable truths: in this lifeless season they are only too bleakly convincing. For this is the winter solstice of the human spirit, the perilous depths of the rising and falling curve in the yearly cycle of our vitality. In the cold and dark, summer is a miracle we cannot believe in—that out of the dead earth will spring coloured flowers, fresh and fragile and sweetly scented. How *can* we belive it possible that we shall cast off clothes and walk out bare-armed in the welcoming warm air? How can we plan for a season which does not exist?

We shrink, we contract the vulnerable spread of living. We are half-way to dying, half-way to drowning in the nights which are a long submergence in darkness. It is a time for emotional hibernation which we should retire to every year as if in preparation for an approaching illness. For it is not this winter only, but every winter: a recurring sickness of the sunless season which is sometimes slight, sometimes near-mortal, but always despairing. For this is the suicide season, the northern dark welling up in our northern souls.

PART FOUR

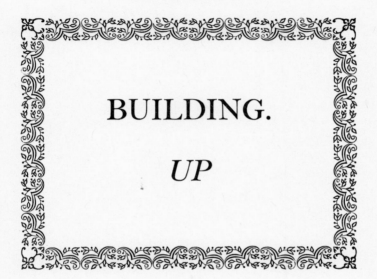

BUILDING.

UP

21

IT IS SPRING AT LAST, SPRING UNMISTAKABLY, warm and growing, with the new grass sprinkled with daisies and the blackthorn in flower in the hedge. In the spring, they said. The builders would start in the spring. On the first warm day, I suppose I imagined, they would arrive complete with bricks and mortar, as anxious as I am to put up the house without another hour's delay. But the blackthorn blossom is here and the builders are not, and my slow-blooded winter resignation has roused to spring fever.

The woods across the valley are changing each day. All winter they have crowned the hills like a landscape in a photograph, a flat two-dimensional pattern of fringed dark branches. But now that the buds are breaking green, the trees stand out from the hill-side like a stereoscopic picture.

In the opposite field a tractor is roaring backwards and forwards over the long rolling hill-side, ploughing last year's stubble in parallel stripes of pale brown earth. At this half-mile distance the sound blows across the open space as a friendly purr, rising and falling as the light wind changes direction. For on this day of spring holiday, even the wind blows idly, with no serious purpose of transporting large volumes of air in the steady direction the meteorologists point out, but only drifting vaguely about this sunshiny hollow in the hills. Black and white birds follow the tractor, rising restlessly and settling again on the new furrows. Gulls certainly, and jackdaws perhaps, but too small to make out at this dazzling bright distance.

Spring is here, but the builders are not. Not here today nor tomorrow nor the day after. In the days of unclouded Easter sunshine the man ploughs steadily, and the strips of turned earth run together to a rough brown surface, which covers the field like a newly shaken rug. But on this side of the valley no one has come to prepare the ground for our house. The field is harrowed and harrowed again, changing the rug to smooth carpet. It is drilled with seed—spring wheat I suppose, watching enviously from our opposite hill-side where nothing is happening.

The petals are falling already from the blackthorn in the hedge, and the builders have not come. In the spring they said. They would start in the spring. And nothing could be more emotionally spring than this warm blue weather with a dozen larks trilling unseen high above me and showering down notes like glancing sequins. For larks are one of the commonest birds of this upland valley, singing all the year round whenever the sun shines, even in winter.

The piles of soil saved from the terrace are green over now with sprouting seedlings, and among the daisies in the field are triumphant yellow dandelions. Across the valley I imagine I can see the new corn shooting already in a faint green dust over the soil which has dried out now to pale grey, smudged here and there with still paler patches where the underlying chalk lies close to the surface.

As the empty days pass there is no mistaking the green of the growing corn, nor the flower-buds in the hawthorn-hedge, and even the new seedlings on the piles of soil are budding out here and there into yellow flowers of charlock. There is a week-end when the beech-trees are suddenly in new leaf, millions and millions of flimsy silk membranes unfolding from the thin stiff twigs. The green is luminous, so delicate and pale it is scarcely darker than yellow, and the trees are translucent, casting no shadows, but filtering the sun through the filmy layers of green, so that the light beneath their branches is not darkened but made more vivid by their living colour. It must be a perilously vulnerable stage in the growth of a tree, and small wonder the fragile leaves so quickly thicken to a serviceable dark-green toughness.

They are darkening already, it will soon be summer, and the builders have not come. Patience is a virtue even more inaccessible than usual: is a word I no longer understand. I seethe with useless frustration, telephone, write letters, go every week-end to call on these phlegmatic men immune to the stirring new season. But even the best of builders have a dozen reasons for not starting building until they are ready. It may even be true, as they assure me it is, that the facing bricks they ordered before Christmas have still not arrived.

But they could dig the foundations, I tell them, and make the drains and put down the concrete. They won't need the facing bricks for weeks yet, I urge them.

Yes, they agree. Yes. That's true enough. There's no doubt they could do all that without facing bricks.

But they do not do it. They do nothing. They sit monumentally solid on their office chairs and my impatience blows over them like the wind. It is as if I tried to move the bull-dozer by pushing: I expend my utmost amount of energy without converting any of it to work. And each time I visit them I come away with the disheartening impression that this is a situation they are perfectly well used to. I suspect that they have listened thus calmly to a hundred equally impatient customers before me, that they are skilled by long experience in avoiding any pressure to begin work before they are ready, and that this is how all builders begin all undertakings—a month at least after the date they agree to.

But we must not begin with ill-feeling. I must strive for a philosophic calm. After all, in a year or two's time in the finished house we shall not even remember so slight a delay in the starting. But I am not calm. I watch the new wheat in the field across the valley, now green unmistakably and beginning already to move in the wind. Later on when the corn is tall, the whole field will sway and flow like water, but today the leafy shoots are only a few inches high, and the movement is only a fleeting brightness across the field's surface. The wind bends the soft grassy growth, and the underside of the leaves shines silver, but between the sparse rows the earth still shows brown and solid, and the passing of the wind is like water sluiced over the ground in a quick flashing film.

On the hill behind me the chiff-chaffs and willow-wrens are back in the hazel-thickets, and the cowslips are over in the grass, which is half-way to mowing height already. Spring they said, and it will soon be summer. Along lavish miles of hedges the hawthorn is creamy-white and almond-scented. But the flowers in procession are mere milestones in my impatience. If the dog-roses blossom round the still-empty field—

But the builders arrive one day when the valley is echoing with cuckoos.

Next Monday, they said. Could I be there first thing Monday morning to see the foreman? They were ready to start if we were, they said. (If we were ready!) They'd bring all their stuff up first thing on Monday and start right away.

It is a week-end of excitement—not suppressed but indulged in—for why should excitement always be denied? A Sunday of unsuppressed jubilation. Tomorrow the house begins: the actual construction of tangible solids for which the last year and more has been only a long preparation of searching and interviewing and negotiating and planning and form-filling and waiting, waiting, waiting. But tomorrow is the real thing, the house itself.

Monday is expectantly fine, with the sun flooding down from a huge empty dome of silvery-blue. Since at eight o'clock it is still only seven by the sun's morning, the dew is still drench-ingly cold in the over-ankle-high grass. But the air is as still as the air in a room, and will soon be as warm. I sit on the edge of the terrace in a dizzy state of happiness and watch my wet feet steam gently in the sun.

The foreman arrives first. We introduce ourselves and shake hands. I say how pleased I am to see him at last. He is non-committal.

It will not be an easy relationship to start with, for he and the workmen must accept me in place of the two-hundred-mile-distant architect, and we must somehow work peaceably to-gether. And workmen dislike women mixed up with their work. They are accustomed to dealing with men, and their usual atti-tude to women in any position of authority is a curious mixture of resentment, condescension, and mistrust. It is simple enough if we meet them singly. As separate individuals the relationship is like any other between two people who get on together more or less well. But in front of their fellows most workmen are acutely conscious of the difference in sex, and any woman in authority offends their manhood. Unless we are wary the first contacts arouse such a storm of opposition that sensible straightforward dealing is impossible. The only thing to do, as I discovered long ago when I worked in hospitals, is to be tactful but to take no notice. For emotional attitudes are less effectively changed by conscious reasoning than by unconscious analogy: if I ignore the emotional tension, then in time so do they. And with the fore-man it is simple—we both want to get the house built as quickly and efficiently as possible. He is here with his whole range of building skills, and I am here with the exact conception of what we want the finished house to be like. They are complementary parts of the same creation, and there is no reason in the world why we should not progress peaceably together.

All of which I ignore by remarking on the fortunate fine weather, which I feel must inspire, even in a confirmed misogy-nist, the sunniest of good temper.

He squints up at the sun and looks round the cloudless horizon.

"Yes," he agrees, "it's a good dry day." There is a pause while he surveys the field. "I like to get moved in in the dry. It makes a good start to a job."

This is progress already, for by country standards between strangers this counts as communicative chatter. Perhaps we are going to be friends straight away and no fuss.

He is a squarish, medium-height man in clothes which are a peculiar compromise between office-desk and building-site, and he has just had a hair-cut so brutally thorough that the back of his head is a bluish stubble. He has an open, earnest, faintly worried face, and the mellow Buckinghamshire accent which always reminds me of newly baked bread.

They were sending us their best man, so the builders told us, and I can well believe it. It was why they were late in starting, they said, because he was finishing another job. Though about that I am not so credulous.

But never mind, here he belatedly is, the essential catalyst who from a mixture of materials and workmen will produce a house. And now that he is safely here the delay already seems insignificant. Spring they said, and hawthorn and cuckoos can certainly count as spring, it was only my impatience which reckoned from the earliest snowdrop.

"I take it you want the house about the middle of that terrace you've levelled out?"

"Yes," I agree.

"Right," he says with an energetic air. "The stuff should be here any minute, and then we'll get going."

Even as we walk back to the gate the first of the lorries roars up the hill from the village and pauses suspiciously at the top of the steep unsurfaced drive. The driver climbs down and looks round approvingly at the view.

"Bit of all right you've got yourself here," he says. He

pushes his cap to the back of his head and rubs his hands together. "Yes. A real bit of all right. I wouldn't mind this myself."

It is a Cockney accent this time, but after all we are less than
forty miles from Bow Bells; the wonder is not that the accents
should meet, but that they should keep their vividly separate
identity.

The foreman has joined the driver who climbs back into his
lorry. "I'd best get this lot clear before Bill arrives—he's right
behind me. Where do I put it, mate?"

It is the first of a convoy of battered lorries which clatter up
all morning with "the stuff"—an enormous paraphernalia of
material and equipment which is unloaded over the site to the
foreman's exact instructions. There is a mixer for concrete, two
huts in sections ready to assemble, and a general assortment of
benches and boards and heavy tools for purposes to me mysterious. There are planks and pipes and scaffolding and ladders, neat
volcano-shaped piles of sand and gravel, square stacks of harsh
red bricks and bags of cement. The lorries roar and labour on
the steep slope, the men shout to each other across the din, the
larks sing ecstatically overhead, and the field looks like a London
street the morning after a night of bombing. But fortunately it
smells far sweeter, for bombed buildings have a peculiar penetrating stench of decay, which haunted the skeleton sites of
London long after the loose rubble was cleared away. But this
is a creative not a destructive chaos, and the piles of new bricks
and damp sand and gravel smell fresh and earthy.

"We'll have the hut there," the foreman says, "up against the
hedge to break the wind behind it. And the carpenter's stuff on
that level bit. And the mixer here, and the plumber's stuff
there."

Despite my first impression of casual dumping the site is laid
out methodically in the flowery grass, like a temporary village.
The foreman's hut goes up at surprising speed, a handsome new
structure which is the Governor's Palace in this summer settle-

ment of workers. There are other huts too, which emerge from the muddle, shabby, much-assembled shelters for cement and tools, and a large communal shed for the workmen's tea-drinking.

The men neither loiter nor hurry, but work steadily at the familiar routine, settling-in and arranging their affairs with a comfortable air of old soldiers campaigning. They have clearly done this dozens of times before, though I silently wonder how they manage in the cramped space of most building-sites, for here they have spread themselves unconcernedly over a most lavish expanse of field.

About my presence on the site the workmen are naturally mistrustful. They are not hostile exactly, but they do not welcome me. And who can blame them? For here I am, an unknown woman from London, only too likely to find fault and interfere (which indeed is what I am here for if put more sympathetically). They would much prefer me to stay in London, and they make their preference clear. For which independence I respect them. Certainly it would be easier to have them neutral, but if I could choose I would rather have them surly than obsequious.

All day the unloading and settling-in goes steadily on, and by tea-time the huts are up and furnished (if it counts as furnishing to balance planks across oil drums for seats and tables). The huts are safe enough I suppose, though they look most alarmingly precarious, with the floors propped level with piles of bricks on the downward slope. The lorries have gone now, gone with some labouring up the drive I anxiously notice, even when empty. But today nothing matters except that the builders have started at last, that from now on any delays will be no more than interruptions of a process which will go on notwithstanding. We have only to wait and watch now, and the house will grow.

Building. *Up*

22

"It is a beauteous evening calm and free" and wonderfully peaceful after the clattering day. For the workmen have departed by lorry and scooter and bicycle, and only the foreman has stayed behind to discuss the plans of the house. He takes off his cap, rubs the top of his cropped head with evident pleasure, then settles his cap again more easily. He too is calm now: it is as if he had let out his breath after holding it in all day.

Now that we're peaceful, he says, will I show him exactly where we want the house to be?

At last. Exactly where. It is what I have waited for all winter and spring: to mark out the site for someone who will straightway set to and build something on it. About the exactly where there is no difficulty, and I show him my enclosure of twigs and stones now firmly trampled into the chalk. That's the front wall of the house, I tell him, and that's the retaining wall of the terrace along the south front.

He surveys this flimsy sketch of a plan without comment. Right, he says, with his odd air of sudden decision. Right. He finds a peg from a pile of scaffolding and rams it hard into the chalk. It is the south-east corner of the house now firmly established. He smiles at me understandingly.

"There. Now are you happy?"

I have made no secret of my impatience all this time: I can scarcely be surprised that he has noticed. I look at the single peg with satisfaction. It is as if the house were some kind of invisible balloon now firmly tethered to this stake.

But the roof is my criterion of a house, not a single peg, and I shall not be satisfied with anything less.

"When will the roof be on?" I ask him.

"Where are we now?" he considers. "End of May is it?" He calculates on his fingers. "June, July, August. We should have the roof on by September. Barring accidents of course" (for people who promise dates are always careful to qualify them).

"And how long before it's finished?"

"Well the roof's about half-way," he says. It is my turn to calculate.

"We shall be in by early next year?"

"You should be—barring accidents."

It is a promise I store away like an unopened present to enjoy later on. Just now there is too much else to think about. I suppose a single corner is all the foreman needs us to decide on as a base to lay out the house, but I long to see the whole plan pegged out before he goes. Tomorrow I shall be back in London. I can't come out again before next week. Has he time? I ask him. Or does he want to get home?

"Alright," he agrees. "Just as you like. I'm not in no hurry, and anyway it might be a good idea to measure it up while you're here—just in case there's any queries. I'll have to ask you to hold the measure, though."

It is not a question of *have* to, I am *delighted* to hold it, to help with the spacing of walls and squaring of corners and checking of levels, consulting the plan, which in any case I know by heart to the last detail.

All trades and skills are fascinating to watch. By the refining of long practice their processes acquire a satisfying elegance and ingenuity, and in watching a skilled workman we are not watching merely the performance of a single individual, but an individual expression of a communal skill perfected by generations of practitioners. Workmen use their skills as we all use the language we could never have invented for ourselves.

As I watch him work I can see why the builders consider this foreman the best of their men. He is thorough and methodical and exact, and although he is never hurried, he is equally never idle. His potential faults will all be to his own disadvantage—

that he might become obsessively conscientious and too easily exploited. I must certainly not ask him again to stay on after hours.

But he seems in no hurry to go, though he has knocked in the last peg now and transferred the house-plan full-size from paper to ground.

"Lucky the level's so true," he says, looking along the terrace. For the driver was right and the terrace is level. This ledge wedged into the hill-side at such an odd-looking angle is a perfect horizontal from back to front. Only along the length of the house does it fall a few inches sideways, for the pegs at the east end are sunk almost down to the chalk surface, while at the west they hold the level strings well above the gently falling ground.

The foreman is satisfied. They can go straight ahead now, he says, and he'll keep any queries till I'm out here again next Monday. "Shouldn't be much to query though. It's a simple enough house. Couldn't be simpler really. You should just see some of the fancy arrangements we're asked to build—in and out and up and down. Never a straight bit of wall or roof anywhere. And plumbing all over the place."

His soft Buckinghamshire voice is deeper now he is calm, and his accent more individual, a vividly organic variation of language, like hand-carved wood after machine-moulded metal. This local accent is more precious by far than the local lace, yet no one bothers to preserve it.

He has folded up the plan now and looks at his watch. It's getting late. He'd best be going. He'll look for me again next Monday, and he'll keep any queries.

He has driven off now down the may-blossom lane and I am left alone on the field with our house-to-be. I stand and survey what is now unmistakably the plan of a building. If my wavering twigs were enough to imply a house, then these square-set pegs and taut levels of string are its exact intellectual confirmation. They no longer merely suggest the idea of some half-vague building, but mark out the exactly square, exactly horizontal area of space which will contain a house of exactly this size and shape.

The human mind has a curious power of projecting continuous surfaces: we need only the indicating lines to supply the planes for ourselves. A fence becomes a wall, rows of arching lamp-standards along a road, however widely spaced, yet make a continuous archway, and the volume of air beneath them is a roofed-over tunnel. They define the space and our mind fills in the gaps. It is why Stonehenge is so powerfully claustrophobic, and why we feel ourselves inescapably imprisoned in its awful circle, even though it is mostly empty air which separates us from the immensities of sky and Salisbury Plain.

So these thin strings stretched above the ground create the floors of a house. And because it is intellectually exact, it is the implied plane of the floors which is real, and the solid surface of the chalk beneath is only a vague approximation which the mind now ignores. And among the flowing shapes of this hill-side the rigid pattern of pegs and strings is strangely alien. It is an inorganic conception which has nothing to do with the landscape, but is unmistakably man's creation. It is like some ghostly vision, a geometric hallucination, and while I look at it the familiar terrace seems suddenly strange, seems not to be simply a surface to which we have added a plan, but an excavation which has unearthed this alien artefact from some different world. We have *discovered* this magic formula for a human house, not created it. And because it is exactly accurate, the pattern has a curious serenity, a dreamy sense of intellectual peace.

The sun is low now along the hill-side, and the level light picks out the foreman's strings in a delicate bright web which is strangely beautiful. But this building of houses is a numinous activity altogether. There is an only half-conscious sense of hidden significances, and atavistic emotions, and ceremonies long ago forgotten. For building shelters to live in must be as ancient almost as the human state: older than agriculture, or living in communities, perhaps even older than the specifically human act of burying the dead, since even animals make shelters to live in. During unknown thousands of years men have concentrated their lives in enclosures which were homes. No wonder the creation of a house is haunted by intimations.

Numinous and therefore in need of ritual. Even in our age of impersonal building methods there are still certain stages which were once so important that even today their ancient ceremonies have not completely vanished—laying the foundation-stone— hoisting the roof-tree. But meaningless formalities now, and the roof-trees of flat-topped London sky-scrapers degenerated to a symbolic barrow-load of concrete, and the distinguished city visitors glad of a warm lift to carry them down to lunch in comfort. As ceremonies now they are meaningless fossils, and even to romantics like me they are no longer even shadows of the lost magic rituals. And in any case I should be sorry to have them back: they would hold up the building and put off the day we moved in.

The air above me is clear now and dark, with the stars beginning, and the arch of the sky is an open window into the blackness of night. The warmth of the day streams out into space —will there be a frost tonight, I wonder, and tomorrow the hawthorn petals brown at the edges? Two hundred feet higher up in the clear night-sky the hill behind me is cold already, and as I walk up to the road the chilled air is beginning to sink down the slope, a silent and secretive sliding, scarcely perceptible as movement, but enveloping me in cold like water. I am glad to shut myself into the car and start back to London, and leave behind me on the dark hill-side the newly born house.

For what the pegged-out plan means to me is quite simple— it is not the ancient elusive household gods who are now firmly tethered, but the even more elusive twentieth-century builders. They are pegged down at last and the house is started.

23

The children once had a mildly educational picture-book about building a house. On every page were coloured drawings of the different stages of construction, and from digging the first neat foundations to putting on the last coat of gleaming paint, every operation was as trim and decorative as afternoon tea in a well-kept garden. The men were very clean, the site was very tidy, the sun was always shining, and the sand and gravel were in piles as exactly symmetrical as Mount Fuji. There was no mess, no litter of any kind in the whole proceedings.

But our house-building is not in the least like that. Judged by picture-book standards our activities are crude and squalid. To an onlooker ignorant of what was happening it would seem less like any form of creation than some scene of violent destruction. For houses, alas, do not grow spontaneously in beauty as trees do. They are constructed by arranging chaos laboriously into order, and so far there is no perceptible ordering of our chaos, but only an increasing mess of ditches and chalk-heaps to add to the general effect of dereliction.

It was not like this in the beginning. The beginning is a civilized business of drawing-boards and blue-prints and the neatly pegged-out plan for me to romance over. Very much a matter of smooth suede shoes in the drawing-room beside this practical business of destructive nailed boots. For this is a dreadful stage of the creation, a harsh and violent birth which I never allowed for in all the houses I built so airily in so many undisturbed green fields. Those early houses sprang up complete like Athene, mellow already and happily merged with their site. Shrubs grew round them from the start, tall trees shaded their smooth established lawns, and their well-worn paths were grown over already with moss at the edges. There was nothing in the least like this crude violence, with trenches everywhere for drains and foundations, and the new summer grass crushed to green pulp, and the meadow flowers buried in sterile chalk, and the trees the bull-dozer wrenched from the hedge broken up now for lighting fires—poor corpses devoured piecemeal.

Each week the chaos increases. It scarcely seems possible that so many glaring piles of chalk like over-sized white mole-hills can all have come out of these narrow trenches. And can the making of concrete and mortar really need such mountains of sand? Can the seemingly endless loads of bricks, which keep on arriving, all be used up in the walls of a single house?

But at least by the end of June the house is emerging. The foundations are solidly laid—solidly enough to dispel even our wary suspicions of possible future trouble. What are we building? one of the workmen asked me. Are we putting up a sky-scraper or something? He'd never done anything so solid before, he said.

For the workmen as well as the foreman accept me amicably now, forgetting their first mistrust of a woman only too likely to interfere. It is a sign of their acceptance that they swear again unconcernedly; not when they talk to me, but among themselves and quite unconcerned whether I overhear. For workmen swear constantly and monotonously, not as an expression of disgust or anger or any other emotion, but simply from laziness, as a way of slowing up the conversation and eking out a limited vocabu-lary. Their swearing is simply undifferentiated language, for no other words are as versatile as those spelt with rows of dots. As for their attitude to me—we have established an easy friendliness based on a repertoire of simple and much-used jokes, which are mostly, of course, on the theme of my ridiculous ignorance about building. The brick-layers find it endlessly funny that I have never heard of frogs in bricks. It will amuse the plumbers to the end that an educated person (for they seem to grant me that with no evidence at all) should not recognize a machine for putting the thread on water-pipes. I imagine they now consider me harmless though useless, and certainly they now greet me cheerfully enough on Monday mornings, accepting me as a weekly variation of the normal working day.

And for this one day a week I share their different life out here on the summer field. For a building-site is not merely a place where men report for work, but a temporary encampment where a group of men live their working-days together. It is not only a house which they build on this hill-side, but also a way of living. And listening to their talk I realize that each job they work on has its own different atmosphere—of good or bad feeling among the men—good or bad fortune in the building operations. There are jobs they remember as a long succession of disasters, others where they felt they were creating a work of art, and tell me with awe how the doors were all moulded oak and the fireplaces made of special Tudor-style bricks. This house they clearly find too starkly plain for their taste, but as a job it seems so far to be going cheerfully enough in a general climate of fair weather.

As the Mondays pass I learn the pattern of their working-day, and recognize its rhythm as much like my own household routine. There are the same periods of hard work and slackness, the energy between the mid-morning break and lunch-time, the *langueurs* of mid-afternoon. There are tasks done willingly, and others put off as long as possible—as in every household; the same small pleasures which decorate the day. I am getting to know too the different personalities of the men: the taciturn solitary who works apart from the others, the pair who work together and keep up a ceaseless argument on the merits of footballers, the excruciatingly bad whistler, and the large unlikely man who won my heart from the beginning by unselfconsciously filling an empty milk-bottle with buttercups and cow parsley he picked in the hedge, and setting it carefully in the middle of the plank they use as a table for their tea-mugs.

Building. *Up*

There is also the Lad. There is always a Lad I discovered, in any working-group, and this one is treated by the men with a tolerant mixture of scorn and affection which shows as a constant friendly buffeting with very mild and mostly quite pointless jokes. The Lad himself is a small, meek curly-haired boy straight from school, who accepts as natural his status as target of rustic wit, and whose only reply to the constant sallies is a wordless and happily embarrassed smile. I have never yet heard him speak.

Just as each workman has a separate character, so also does his work. For each works to one standard only, both for speed and performance. They are like engines with a fixed natural pace, which may be either fast or slow but does not vary to suit the circumstances. And their performance too is of a consistent quality; whether slap-dash or thorough they do not adjust it to suit the job they are given. To get a different standard of work we must choose a different man, for it is no use asking a rough worker to do some particular task with care: he does not control his slap-dashery to order. Nor will a meticulous worker hurry through some unimportant job and get it done roughly. No matter how we hurry him he will white-wash the tool-shed as carefully as he papers the drawing-room. It is as if the men as working entities were self-propelling machines not controlled by the discriminating brain. They do not make the effort to connect the two together into a flexible and therefore more efficient working instrument. That is the foreman's job: to choose the right man for the right task and put his complicated working machine into the right gear for what it has to do.

In this working community the Dog (even more than the Lad) is light relief. It is the same black Labrador which has taken a neighbourly interest in our affairs from the start, and it lives down the lane, I discovered, in a house of oldish people. How it passes the time when no one is building in the valley I can't imagine, since this house now engrosses its whole day. For workmen building houses are a very different matter from a solitary stranger in a field, and it joined the party on the day of their first arrival, coming through the hedge inquiringly as the first lorry came down the drive. It chose a vantage point on the field at a distance from the noisy operations, and sat down to watch with its large black tail spread straight out behind like a kangaroo. Apart from a break for lunch (or so I suppose, for it went off through the hedge at lunch-time and came back half-an-hour later), it sat there all day, watching this new activity in a long-empty field with an intelligent, contemplative air. It never moved from its chosen spot, nor showed the slightest surprise at anything that happened, and only if someone addressed it, thumped its black tail on the earth with a slapping thud without getting up.

That was the first day of the acquaintance, and now it is an accepted member of the community. It sits in its home garden (so the workmen tell me with pride, as if it were a performing animal they had trained themselves) and watches the road for their lorry to pass. Then it jumps up at once and goes off on its short-cut through the hedge to greet them on the site as they come down the drive. It is everyone's friend now, but still an animal of most sedate and exquisite manners. It never romps, never barks, and its only peculiarity is an insatiable passion for sticks. Not only for sticks as we normally mean them—pieces of branch that we fling out to sea for our dogs to recover—but for anything even remotely stick-like, from mere over-size twigs to lengths of plank too heavy to move. It will rush off and fetch a stick from any distance, or dig one out furiously from great heaps of rubbish the workmen pile on top to tease it. Sticks are a wild excitement in this dog's life, but sticks apart, it moves with most delicate precision, controlling its awkward bulk as consciously as a cat. It never trips over strings or knocks down tools, and it seems to know by some extra sense exactly which concrete is wet and must not be walked on.

Naturally the workmen have adopted it with enthusiasm,

and it shares their tea-breaks in the hut with equal satisfaction. It has its own mug in the window-sill row of enamel veterans battered and stained from years of making tea and rinsing out in buckets. The bell rings for tea. The dog jumps up and hurries expectantly to the door of the hut before anyone else has even laid down his tools. (It would be an excellent dog for Pavlov's experiments and, with a little patience, could no doubt be trained to keep its own records as well.) It likes plenty of sugar in its tea, so the men tell me approvingly, and in return for the lavish sugar it amuses its audience with ridiculous bouts of sneezing when the tea is too hot. And this is the best joke in the world. The men guffaw with laughter, slap their dusty knees with enormous hands, and rock unconcernedly to and fro on their precariously balanced planks.

And like the dog I too have my routine in this life of the building-site. Over the family week-end we all of us examine the house and I write down the things to discuss with the foreman. On Monday morning I arrive with my list, and the foreman meets me with a similar list of his own, which he produces from a pocketful of papers. For even with the most detailed plans and specifications it is surprising how many questions arise each week.

We walk round the building together, drawing cryptic illustrations on odd bits of wood or the backs of our lists, and bigger diagrams on patches of concrete with lumps of the ubiquitous chalk. The foreman's hair has grown to a reasonable length again I notice (there is plenty of time to notice, for we never hurry), and the back of his head no longer emerges below his cap like a badly shaved face. We sit down comfortably now on the rising foundations to go through our lists, and check off the separate items at his conscientious pace. It is very peaceful, like being in a boat on a calm sea. For miles around us the fields lie green and smiling and the air is warm with summer, the man's soft country voice is a country sound like the fainter sounds of the valley, and all the time, across the enormous sky behind his head, majestic summer clouds move slowly past in glorious progression.

At this early stage of the building there is nothing much to discuss at length. We have finished by the time the bell rings for tea, and Yes, I assure the now friendly workman who brings me my scalding half-pint in the most presentable of their battered mugs, Yes. That is just how I like it. For how can I ask for weak tea and no sugar, without seeming to find fault with all the previous cups of sticky-sweet toffee-brown brew they have brought me each Monday?

"Nice day," the man says, looking round the sunny land-scape as if he had only just noticed. Is he waiting for the mug back I wonder? But the tea is too hot to swallow down all at once whatever good manners may demand, and he seems in no hurry.

"When I was a lad," he says companionably, "we used to come nutting up this valley. A whole bunch of us. Come every year we did—at the back-end. Quite a thing it were too, going nutting. Used to beat down the bushes with sticks to get at 'em. You could always tell when boys was out nutting—could hear 'em miles off." He stops to remember, listening for the vanished boys perhaps on the hill-side behind us. Then he goes on again.

"A deal more woodland there was too in them days. All the stretch between here and the village—all thick wood it was—no fields. Red squirrels there was too—not the grey rats you see nowadays, but red uns—lots of 'em—all between here and the village."

He stops again and I sip my tea in no hurry to finish, and wait for him to go on.

"A good lot of changes though there's been in these parts since I was a lad. A powerful lot. I recollect when that lane along the bottom was full of springs—dozens of 'em—breaking out all along the bank. And smothered with fern. Like a grotter it was all along the bottom there. And the ditches running water all summer through. And now it's dry as a bone—no sign of water. I reckon it's the war what did it. That war brought a powerful lot of changes, and not for the better neither."

He stops to consider the bad-to-worse world and I sip my diminishing tea by thimblefuls.

"Have you always lived here?" I ask him, to start the talk off again.

"Yes," he says proudly. "Born in the house next-door where we are now. Never lived away—and wouldn't want to neither —I reckon you're best where you're used to."

If we are to begin a philosophic discussion on the virtue of roots I am certainly not the one to argue with him, though even to me his near-vegetable immobility does perhaps seem excessive.

But he is not going to begin a discussion this morning on roots or anything else. He has finished. He has talked already far longer than I have ever heard him before, and now quite clearly his only interest is whether I have finished my tea and will give him my mug. Today, alas, I shall hear no more on the fascinating subject of These-parts-when-I-was-a-lad.

⊰⊱ *24* ⊰⊱

In any journey there are three separate and recognizable stages. First there is the setting-out, the more-or-less anxious business of organizing the expedition and getting it off complete and on time. Then there is the journey itself, with its satisfying sense of achievement in each mile travelled. This is the most peaceful stage for the travellers, since we hand ourselves over as so much baggage to be passively transported. Even in a motor-car which we drive ourselves we are only a part of the steering-wheel:

we have only to propel the car; and even driving across London in the rush hour is wonderfully soothing compared, for instance, with getting a family off on summer holiday.

The third stage of the journey is less definite and more variable. It begins imperceptibly as we near the end, and we can recognize the transition by a growing impatience to arrive. We are no longer travelling, but impatiently covering the distance which still separates us from where we want to be. However it is not the number of miles remaining which decides our impatience: it is their proportion of the whole. On a journey of fifty miles, impatience is high by forty-nine, but on a journey of a hundred miles, at forty-nine we are still placid travellers.

In the building of this house we are now safely off and have travelled about a quarter of the journey. The anxieties of starting are well behind us, and the prospect of finishing still too far away to make us impatient. We have handed the transporting over to the builders, and our only part in the journey is to choose minor variations of the route.

The summer settles down to a crowded but unexpectedly peaceful rhythm. Certainly there is more going on than usual, but the framework is much as it has always been, and untroubled now by the anxious frustration of the spring setting-out. And every week-end, whether on Friday night or Saturday morning, there is a culminating moment at the end of the journey from London, when we arrive at the site and see what the builders have done in the week of our absence. The emotion is an irresistible blend of curiosity, expectation, satisfaction, jubilation, and a wonderfully pleasant sense of creation.

For the rest of the family I think it is curiosity simply: a mere brief visit of inspection. When the house is finished they are ready enough to move in and live there, but meanwhile these creative stages are the builders' concern not theirs. Their visit is scarcely more than an intelligent interest in the general process of putting up a building.

Building. *Up*

But for me it is not general at all: it is personal creation. *We* are building the house, and the workmen are the elaborate and highly skilled tool we are using to do it. Nor is it only a house we are making, but a new way of life which I now look forward to as if to some idyllic holiday existence, and which every week grows visibly closer. Each brick laid is a small achievement, a strip of concrete is an active satisfaction, and a new length of drain is as pure a pleasure as a new rose in flower for the first time.

And the drains and foundations are finished now: the walls have begun to rise. Already there are several rows of bricks on the concrete footings, enclosing the house and rising between the rooms like the rims of shallow dishes holding the slabs of the concrete floors like slabs of grey toffee. They are scarcely walls yet, scarcely more than outline rows of bricks, but still they are unmistakably the rooms to be. Certainly they are definite enough to dismay us by their tiny size: a well-known stage which alarms all inexperienced builders of houses. Can this really be what we asked for? Are these tiny enclosures the rooms we imagined? They are absurdly small—mere dolls'-house size. No one but a family of pygmies could hope to inhabit them in comfort.

But everyone, so the foreman assures us, is equally dismayed at the smallness of his half-built house, no matter how spacious it will finally be. Is it perhaps that our imagination always magnifies, as our memory does in scenes from our childhood? Perhaps. But I think it is rather that an unfinished house does not sufficiently enclose us in its own small scale of space, so that we judge it, not in terms of rooms, but by the larger scale of the world outside. A finished house is a separate environment which we enter both mentally and physically when we pass through the door, and without any conscious adaptation we alter our values to suit our changed surroundings. Because we expect a house to be warm, an unheated house seems colder than out of doors. As we walk in through the doorway the air seems actually physically colder, however clearly a thermometer proves that the temperature is exactly the same. And equally because we expect the inside of a house to be dark, a sunny room surprises us by its lightness. How bright this room is, we feel, even though we have just come in from the sunlight outside which is many times brighter. And size is the same: a room seems large or small because we judge it by an unconsciously accepted average size for rooms and find it larger or smaller.

But the divisions of a half-built house are not yet rooms, they are projected enclosures indicated by rows of bricks on the ground. They are not separate volumes of space which surround us with their own scale of value, but tiny areas of the site compressed in brick frames and judged by the size of the whole building area. This is what everyone warned us of beforehand, this dismay at the match-box-sized rooms. And reassurance is easy. These tiny constricting cells are much the same size as the rooms we are living in now. We have only to measure and confirm. They will be big enough when once we experience them as the rooms of a house instead of as tiny plots in a seven-acre field.

The week-ends now are divided between pottering happily about the growing house and keeping the Regency Villa tidy for prospective buyers. In all the seven years that we have lived in it our villa has never been so well-cared for. It has never before looked even remotely like a setting for gracious living, as it now quite surprisingly does if living graciously is what the next owners want. For I converted my last spring's impatience to finishing off the cleaning and decorating, and we now live in the unnatural state of the whole house refurbished together. It is a condition quite alien to our ordinary domestic existence, for my usual method of spring-cleaning is a simple leap-frog system of redecorating the dirtiest room, which then becomes the cleanest. But in the Regency Villa now *every* room is clean, every shed and store-room is clear of rubbish. I have papered the attic with ivy wall-paper, the dining-room with stripes. I have painted the kitchen and distempered the scullery and pantry and washed all the paint of the house from top to bottom and front to back.

Already various people have been to look over it, but none of them has liked it enough to want it, and who are we to blame them?—It is too near the road they say—No central-heating —Not enough bedrooms. I have learnt to restrain myself from pointing out a host more objections they may not have noticed, but William is not restrained at all, and points them out feel-ingly. The rooms are sunless, he tells them. There is too much staircase. It is cold in winter. There is no near-by country. He enlarges on the villa's shortcomings with a fine disregard of our chances of selling it. But someone will like it, so the agent assures us. We have only to wait. Someone will see it as exactly what they have always been looking for. It is that sort of house, he says. We can only hope he is right, and that this mythical some-one will arrive before the new house is finished.

Meanwhile we keep ourselves clean and tidy and uneasily ready for inspection, inside and out. If I looked after the house, so I insisted, then the others should look after the grass. It is not so much fair, since they are three and I am one, but it is the only help likely to be useful. So they mow the grass—lawns and long grass and edges—and the garden has never looked so much like a public park. If we weeded the flower-beds we could open it officially and charge a shilling for the nurses. For despite our half-hearted trimming of the elaborate box-hedges, it really is a good garden, laid out in the nineteenth century when the park which once surrounded the house was turned into farmland, and it was designed, so they say in the village, by the landscape gardener who laid out the Rothschild parks.

It is only that we are not interested in well-tended gardens. Our hearts—no, *my* heart, for the others are heart-whole still —is already away on the hill-side, and if I had nothing else to do I would put up a tent and stay there all summer. However the

London week of absence has the very real advantage that every Saturday visit to the building-site there is a most noticeable advance. There is a week-end when the walls are a foot or so high and the windows held in position: a delightful but fleeting stage to enjoy while it lasts, like the flowering of cherries. We sit on the foot-high walls with our feet in the living-room and look out through the window-frame. We are conscious now of the room as an entity, but we are still out of doors—an intriguingly double experience.

And now that the house is past the foundation stage the discussions with the foreman grow more interesting Monday by Monday. We talk about doorways now instead of drains, and how many bricks high we want the terrace wall, and how large a flower-bed we want left open in the floor of the conservatory —entrancing topics which I draw out happily till mid-morning tea. And after tea I leave them, for it scarcely seems tactful to stay about the house while the men are working: they could hardly help feeling they were being inspected (which of course they would be).

Across the valley the wheat-field is already changing colour, a vivider green in the jig-saw cover of fields, and shaded like shot-silk where the new stalks of the growing corn are bloomed with blue. It is the exact stage where *le blé en herbe* changes to the young corn springing. Each week it grows higher, grows paler, warms with the coming gold of harvest. And as the corn grows so does the house. Every week-end now is a noticeable stage further on the journey home, and one milestone Saturday we arrive to find that the first-floor joists are up and the ground-floor rooms enclosed.

For the first time now we are conscious of the rooms as places. Until now they were mere indications of what we intended, but these are actual rooms, particular enclosures with their own separate identity in the co-ordinated grouping of spaces which is a building. We can walk in now at the door and

Building. *Up*

at once feel ourselves contained in a house: the proportions are perfectly clear and the volumes significant, simply because they are roofed in. Before they were merely a larger version of the plan of the house on paper, but now they are the living-rooms of a habitable house.

And because it is separate now from the outside world with its different scale, the house is suddenly astonishingly larger. The rooms are almost spacious now: there is no feeling of being cramped in boxes, but only of moving serenely through the hollow volumes of linked enclosures without restriction. At last we can see what the finished house will be like and it is wonderful: it is just as we hoped it would be. For till now we could never be sure. Were the paper plans really a translation of our visionary intentions, or would the house be only a disappointing approximation? But we are not disappointed. This is indeed what we intended: a house which will firmly enclose us in its own strong sense of identity, yet which never for a moment shuts us off from the surrounding country. The landscape is an extension of every room, and the house is full of bird-song and the smell of trees and flowers—which is scarcely surprising since there is no glass in the windows, nor ceiling to the rafters, and the airs of summer drift through like an open cage.

But the house has emerged in essentials, and we all of us recognize this hot July week-end as a milestone. I think it is the first time the others have felt that this is their own house where they themselves will actually live, and not simply an impersonal exercise in building methods. William stands by the window-frame of his study-to-be. "I can put my chair here," he says. "The view's magnificent. Come and see." His voice is delighted but it is also surprised. He is telling me news. Until today I think he never realized that he himself would sit and walk and sleep and wake inside these walls: that his own intimate personal life would be changed by this house we are building.

The boys too are newly engrossed, and walk in and out of

the rooms as if savouring an unexpected new experience, and I feel I am welcoming them all to a house where I have been living for months already. Not that I have lived here alone, for the others have been my constant companions, familiar inhabitants already in this house which so irresistibly invites our lives to its own confident pattern. And because this house is different from the one we are leaving, our life here will be different too. The rhythm of the day will be changed, leisure will have an altered emphasis as well as work, and the small familiar pleasures, like flowers in the daily routine, will grow here in different places.

It is evening now and the others have gone, and I sit so still on this quiet hill-side that the bats flitter as close to my unmoving head as if I were part of the scaffolding. An empty house is a vacuum which draws in human lives, and since we do not yet occupy these rooms in solid flesh and blood, they are haunted again tonight by the ghosts of the future. As I walk through the shadowy house I half-expect to find the rooms already occupied by their peaceful presences—men who look up without surprise from the book they are reading, quiet women who smile to greet me. For they too must love this house or they would not live here, and since they do we are friends. And because our intimate lives are shaped by the same mould of this house, we understand each other more closely than acquaintances met every day. The same things are familiar to us, the same rooms and windows and doorways: even our unconscious movements are adapted to the same spaces, and if we walked in our sleep our mindless bodies would know their way equally well about this same familiar house.

At this half-finished stage of the building their phantom occupation is scarcely more nebulous than our own, and in the evening half-light they are as real as I am, no stranger than the bottomless purple-blue sky between the rafters, nor the bats flickering black through the empty window-frames.

Building. *Up*

◇◇◇◇◇ *25* ◇◇◇◇◇

But the summer is not all sun and satisfaction. August is a month of storms, constant and violent storms sweeping in from the south-west and breaking against the hill-side. Our famous uninterrupted view is a view of uninterrupted bad weather. The sky rains deluge, the water floods down the hill behind us, gathers to a lake on the level of the road, then rushes in a steep river down the unsurfaced drive, eroding gullies like canyons, and washing away my optimism in torrents of muddy white water.

I am back at the bottom of my emotional seesaw, drowned in despair as the country is drowned in rain. "Fools build houses" —it is the recurring refrain of my depressions, and now it seems the many counsellors were right after all, and not the mere unadventurous wet-blankets we dismissed them for. With every black storm which sweeps over the valley I am more damply convinced of our folly.

For the poor roofless house is a watery ruin and the rooms are a series of paddling-pools. The bad-tempered workmen sweep them out between storms, but before they can finish the rain fills them level again, and the ground near the house is churned to a pale glistening paste of white mud crossed precariously by duck-boards. The building stops. Nothing can be done till the weather changes, and the men are sent off to other, indoor jobs. They will never come back. The rain will never stop. The house will never be finished but will moulder to a roofless ruin like an abandoned folly. I sink to a dull wretchedness uncomforted by any patient reasoning that since the house is started it will certainly be finished. I tell myself confidently that with the roof once on it will dry out again in a week or two of fine weather and that in a year from now this quagmire will be only a piquant memory in our dry and completed state.

So I tell myself as fact incontrovertible. But I do not believe it: I am not reassured. For although Oscar Wilde (or was it Whistler?) no doubt meant us to take it ironically when he said he was not convinced by mere fact, yet he only stated the simple truth. For although our intellect is commonly swayed by our emotions, our emotions are seldom controlled by our intellect.

Certainly this weather is far more convincing than any reasoning I can produce. Thunder grumbles and mutters below the horizon, encircling us with menace. The sky is solid purple with storm, and I sit disconsolately in the shelter of the car, watching the clouds move over the valley from the opposite hills, trailing their ragged grey fringes of falling rain. There is nothing I can do but go away like the men and forget about houses until the heavens see fit to stop raining down floods.

I set off back through the stormy twilight, and as if I drove into fog I drive into densest melancholy. For travelling at dusk is always dangerous for anyone not sheltered by cheerful preoccupations. There is a strange mood of sadness which lies in wait for all those who travel alone through the failing light; we are lost and lonely, straying forlorn in a grey world between day and dark. At twilight all creatures who travel abroad are homeless, and on the familiar road I am a stranger in an alien country.

But the day is too stormy for twilight to last. Under the low roof of clouds the dark comes early, and the dark is different. For the night is not sad but mysterious, is travelling across the bed of an ocean with the sky as fathomless dark water above us. Nearer London now, and the sky glows orange over the miles of bright city. Beyond the dark fields is a chain of lights which are the first outlying street-lamps, and as I appraoch them the green of their distant view changes steadily to white. The wet roads shining, the cars splashing, the wind tossing trees in suburban gardens—London is cheerful again. I am glad to be back.

And indeed it is time that I did come back to catch up with all the housekeeping extras put off from week to week all through the summer of fine weather. It will need to rain for a month at least if I am to make up the arrears which steadily gather when my working-week is reduced to a four-day Tuesday to Friday.

And for a month it rains without ceasing. The well-washed London pavements shine with wet, and whenever I go to the door the space of the street between the rows of high houses is slanted with falling showers. Day after day the milkman's hair is plastered down dark with rain, the postman fumbles with letters under his dripping cape, and outside the windows disgruntled passers-by are hunched beneath umbrellas.

But for all that there must have been dryer intervals that I never noticed, for one week-end when we go to look at the derelict house (philosophically now, resigned to despair, disciplined to a new-found patience), there, miraculously, as if it had grown in the damp like a mushroom when no one was looking, the roof is on.

Not the tiles yet, but the timbers for the tiles: the long firm ridge like a keel, and the sloping beams like the ribs of an upturned boat. It is only a matter now of a few fine days of tiling, so the foreman reassures us, then the house will be sealed off from the weather and work can go on under cover no matter what happens outside.

On the end of the roof is a branch of green leaves, which I think must be meant as a modest hint that this is a crucial stage which should rightly be celebrated. (On the way back through the village I must remember to leave word for a crate of beer to be sent up for the workmen.) But I need no beer to celebrate so notable an achievement, for with the roof in position hope comes flooding back. The house is no longer a vulnerable ruin abandoned to watery decay, but a half-made building which experienced men are working on in the confident knowledge that it will be finished and ready for us to move in before spring. The whole emotional climate has changed in ten minutes: the sun shines again from a cloudless sky—and all the usual rest.

But I rejoice too soon. Next Monday the roof-tiles have

come and the tilers are ready to start. But the tiles are wrong. Utterly and horribly wrong. They will have to be changed.

So far our labour-relations have been increasingly amiable, but the roof is a major crisis, aggravated for both sides by the weeks of delay in the building time-table. It was months ago when William and I chose the tiles to go with the bricks, and so that there should be no possible mistake I gave the builders not only the name of the makers and the exact colour we wanted, but also a sample tile to check by. And now this Monday, piled up ready for the tilers to start, are hundreds and hundreds of tiles of a violent bluish-purple, equally horrible with bricks and sky and hill-side.

I rush to the foreman. The tiles are wrong. What happened?

They're the colour we asked for, he says, defensively, only supplied by a different firm.

But the colour we asked for they quite certainly are *not*, whatever name the firm may see fit to call them by. They will not do. (I am shocked into truculence.) We insist on the ones we ordered. But the foreman is truculent too, and since he is in the wrong, he is also bad-tempered.

There's a six-week delay for the ones we ordered, he says. (But why weren't they ordered six *months* ago?) So they got the same colour from another firm. (They are *not* the same colour—it is no use him repeating it. I produce my own sample tile to prove it.)

The foreman changes his tactics. The tilers are here, he says, waiting to start. (Then they must go away again.) If we wait for the other tiles then we shan't get the house by next spring.

But this is straightforward blackmail and only makes me crosser. If we never have a roof on the house at all *we won't have those tiles*. Six weeks or six months, I tell him, we simply don't care. We insist on the tiles we ordered.

The foreman is mutinous, but so am I. And though we shall certainly win in this battle of the roofing, he can easily make it a

Building. *Up*

Pyrrhic victory by holding things up indefinitely. And I have no intention of waiting six weeks.

How many tiles does he need? I ask him.

He tells me, but sulkily.

I tell him nothing, but go back to the car and drive off in a furious roar of mounting gears. The factory that makes the tiles is no more than fifty or sixty miles away—I will go and get them myself. I work out the way on the map and set off cross-country. There is no question of being reasonable: frustration, impatience, bad temper, horror at the purple roof—all are fused to the simple intention of getting the right tiles by next Monday. I am determined (or obstinate might be the better word, for obstinacy is determination grown on poor ground, and the colour of our roof can scarcely count as one of the world's worthier causes).

I am obstinate then, and I cover the sixty awkward country-lane miles in a single-minded fury which carries me without check through factory gates, through yards and corridors and waiting-rooms (if anyone tried to stop me I never noticed) into some holy of holies of manager's office. Out pours the story in an irresistible flood—the house, the builders, the rain, the despair, the tilers, the horrible purple (he has no chance, poor man, to interrupt), and please will he send us the proper tiles before next Monday?

He leans back and whistles. "That's a tall order you know. Do you realize what you're asking? We've not only got to *make* the tiles, but those particular ones are then dipped in acid to weather them. Even if we put them in hand right away as an express order, they'd take a week to finish—let alone deliver, and anyway there's a six-week delay for a start."

He is judicious, explicit, reasonable, and also amused. But I am none of these things: I am only determined (there is now no worthier cause than the colour of roofs). I arrange his working-week. He can start the tiles this afternoon, I tell him, they'll be finished by the week-end, then the lorry can deliver them first thing on Monday morning.

It is not only astonishing that he listens, but even more astonishing that I take it for granted he will. But perhaps all miracles happen simply because nobody doubts them. And on Monday the tiles are there—greyish, sanded, weathered already—they delight me as much as they surprise the foreman: surprise and annoy and relieve him all at once, a curious emotion to watch.

Even in the bitterest quarrel we feel more kindly towards an enemy we have worsted, and the foreman is not in the least my enemy. I have not quarrelled with *him* but only with his tiles, and now I am rid of them I love him dearly. But this is no day to seem to exult in my unfair victory. Today only the briefest of visits, then back to London to leave him a week to recover his natural good temper.

By the following Monday the tiles are on and the tilers have vanished. The roof is discreetly and safely grey, and its colour is never mentioned again by either of us.

◇◇◇◇◇ 26 ◇◇◇◇◇

We are most of us so naturally perverse that things we decide to get rid of seem suddenly precious, and places we are leaving, suddenly attractive, as if we could only appreciate what we are losing. It has happened to me so often that I long ago learnt to harden my heart beforehand; but it has not happened with the Regency Villa. There is no need of heart-hardening, for we have sold it, and without a pang.

The family who are buying it fell in love at first sight, exactly as the agent promised; so thoroughly and blindly in love that we felt ourselves responsible for their infatuated state, and dutifully described the unexpected inadequacies of the house as a partner for everyday living with after the honeymoon. But they smiled aside our warnings of sunless windows and cupboardless bedrooms and keeping the roof clear of snow, knowing as soon as they walked in from the pagoda-roofed veranda that this was the house they had searched for for years. I daresay no one ever fell out of love for hearing that the loved one was bad-tempered at breakfast, and certainly the new owners are undismayed by anything we tell them. Yes, they can see there's a lot of staircase to warm in winter. No, they don't mind the bedrooms being small. And the garden's beautiful, and the extra pantry will make a study, and they'll put another bath under the stairs, and the view from the east windows is wonderful, and everyone they meet in the village is extraordinarily friendly, and they like the road close by, and they don't mind the traffic, and they don't want to live in the country.

To argue with the converted only entrenches them in their convictions. (Even William's gloomy warning to expect dry rot again in the kitchen floor scarcely checks their enthusiasm.) Besides, why should we argue? If our reasons for not liking the house are their reasons for liking it, as it seems they are, then what could be more convenient?

But what if no one had liked it? Should we have had to sell the new house instead? It is a possibility too dreadful to consider, and certainly we never did. And now it is only a matter of the formal arrangements, legal processes which this time seem mercifully slow since they give me time for packing up and putting our furniture away in store in the village, and us away in London for the winter till the new house is ready next spring.

The weeks pass with no emotion but boredom with this long-drawn-out process of disposing of a house we long ago decided to leave. But the formalities are settled at last. We are ready. The van comes. We pack. We leave. Except as another milestone passed on the way to the new house it is a scarcely registered experience. But then we left the Regency Villa in spirit more than a year ago, and in any case, since we never settled, the removal is less like uprooting a way of life than leaving an hotel with an inordinate amount of luggage.

However, even considered merely as hotel, the loss of the Regency Villa leaves a most inconvenient gap. There is nowhere now to stay overnight in the country, and though I may not be conscious of leaving a house we have more or less lived in for seven years, I am very conscious of losing the week-ends spent with the new house in building. My weekly visits now are no longer solitary communings with a future hill-side life on leisurely Sunday mornings, but a brief visit on Monday to see the foreman and get back to London before the rush hour. I launch the family on their working-day then get off myself as fast as I can to the country. The arrival is still an excitement, and with every absent week's progress the house is a noticeable stage nearer to our moving in. It is like going to sleep on a long train journey then waking up to look out of the window and see how much further we have travelled to our destination.

The house is safely enclosed now against the autumn weather, with glass in the windows as well as tiles on the roof. For the workmen like shelter and don't in the least share our enthusiasm for an unenclosed house. Even with glass in the windows they still feel exposed.

"What do you think of it, Bert, all this glass? Not what I'd fancy myself I must say." It is proof of their acceptance of my presence that they talk to each other as if I were not there. I suppose since they mostly see me pottering about the future garden in clothes as shabby as their own, they must think of me as a fellow-worker. Certainly they feel themselves under no constraint to praise the house they are building for us.

"No, I don't fancy it neither. Like living in a gold-fish tank. I'd rather be private myself." Though what they think will invade their precious privacy in this empty field I can't imagine, except the sun by day and the moon by night. And anyway *we* like it: like it better indeed every week as it grows to a finished house. Private from the country world outside is exactly what we do not want to be. All the birds of the air can spy on our innocent domestic lives if they care to. And besides, it is not our human privacy which this house lays open, but the intimate life of the country outside. *We* shall be the ones who spy, who will lie in bed and share the preoccupied early-morning lives of night-hungry birds, who will watch a farm-labourer starting up his tiny tractor on the opposite hill-side while we drink our morning coffee, or who will look up from our evening book as a fox glides out from the hedge and pauses to watch some movement in the shadowy valley before he slinks off down the hill. (I have watched him already.)

How leisured our future life here looks from this idealizing distance, as if our days would be nothing but a long sitting-about and looking. It scarcely seems likely, but still it is a vision of imagined ease which comforts me like a vision of paradise through this long unleisure. Though the worst is over now, with the Regency Villa gone and the new house reduced to a brief weekly outing. But these Monday visits can't compare with the enchanted Saturday arrivals when the growing house stood there empty and waiting to welcome us for the week-end. Now there is no peaceful inspection of the future rooms, but only a cursory and seeming indifferent survey of the week's progress. With the men at work it is scarcely tactful to linger, and the house now belongs to the builders. It is only as much ours as the furniture is ours stored away by the removal-men to winter in their warehouse. The house is inhabited by workmen, and I am a mere brief visitor.

Even the men seem to feel my homeless state and have given me a place of my own.

"We've cleared out that end room," they tell me one Monday (it is William's study), "and put all your stuff together so you'll know where to find it."

My "stuff" is a decrepit assortment of garden tools, much-thumbed plant-catalogues, old coats and Wellington boots; the only object anyone could claim with pride is my brother's leather-cased tape-measure. This shabby collection is neatly arranged in a row along one wall, and the rest of the floor is unnaturally empty: no brick-chippings, no blobs of mortar, no nails, no shavings or ends of wood—nothing but brush-marks in the dust, like raked sand in a Japanese garden, where someone has carefully swept it more or less clean for my occupation. This is now my Monday home. There is no door yet, but there is glass in the window and a window-sill to sit on. And certainly no one will disturb me in here unless they must. The workmen will now be nervous coming in without warning, as if I could never possibly be doing anything else but changing all my clothes down to the most intimate layers. How they will manage with no door to knock on I cannot imagine, but I am sure their tact will be absolute, for most workmen I have ever met have instinctive and sensitive good manners. Unless I leave my sanctuary for the neutral territory of the rest of the house I doubt whether they will even bring me my usual mug of tea, which grows each week more sugary as the men grow more friendly.

"Late today, ain't you? We feared you'd met with some misfortune mebbe. Nasty that London road is. Very. Wouldn't care to drive on it meself I must say. However we've kept your tea hot against your coming." And he produces a mug kept tepid rather than hot by a tile on top, and he hands it to me in welcome. Its brown surface swims with a film of cement dust, and I drink it down appreciatively in the spirit it is offered.

The other men greet me and we go through our established repertoire of jokes to confirm our friendly relations, then I slip off to inspect the house discreetly while they are still in the hut with the dog drinking tea. After that the foreman and I settle down to our Monday business of going through our lists of questions. They are increasingly long lists now as the developing building becomes specialized into a finished house; for at the beginning the questions were only for me as more-or-less ignorant representative of the distant architect, not for me as occupying housekeeper; but each week now they come closer to my domestic concerns as the house comes closer to our domestic occupation.

Will I go to the builders' merchants and choose the washbasins and lavatory and bath?

Do we really want a pot sink and teak draining-boards and not stainless steel?

What tiles do we want for the outside window-sills? (He is wary of tiles now.)

And what about floors?

Yes. What about them? For floor surfacing and built-in cupboards were part of the cargo we dropped overboard at the very beginning to save our new house-building boat from sinking. Since then an unexpected cheque from my American publishers has retrieved the cupboards and bookshelves, but as whitewood cupboards made to measure seem to cost more than solid mahogany bought in a shop, the floors must wait. No doubt the worst of the voyage is over now and we are still fairly safely afloat, but nonetheless the floors must wait.

So concrete screed downstairs, I tell the foreman firmly, and plain boards up. He makes no comment, but I think we lose status badly by not having the polished parquet he describes so proudly from the last house he built. "Right throughout," he says. "Lovely. Every inch over. No end of a job it was too, getting the squares exactly right at the back of the lavatory pan."

But I fear that we constantly disappoint him. For he is most touchingly anxious to build us a fine house, and we are equally anxious to keep it plain. Certainly we appreciate his concern, but certainly it would all be much easier to manage if he were merely indifferent. For his ideas of betterment are not ours, and most Mondays I am faced with the delicate and unpleasant task of asking for some embellishment to be removed without too much hurting his feelings. And since I am naturally cowardly some are never removed at all. I notice an unnecessary angle, a moulding that should be flush, some carpentry pointlessly complicated that could be simple. Shall I say something? Certainly it would be easy enough to alter it at this half-finished stage, but to ask for it different is to criticize his taste; and about our own taste we are all most awkwardly sensitive.

I work myself up. I tell myself that hurt feelings will quickly recover, whereas bad design will survive for generations to annoy everyone who notices. I tell myself I must be responsible as the architect's representative. But it only sometimes works. Certainly the major offences are dealt with, but there is a sprinkling of minor deformities which the house will always bear as tokens of the foreman's taste and my cowardice.

I suppose all periods have looked back to some former time as a lost Golden Age. Certainly it is a process which starts so surprisingly early in history that it seems to be a natural human instinct quite independent of any facts. The Garden of Eden itself is a convenient all-purpose model of Utopia, easily adapted to any country simply by changing the species of the Tree of Knowledge. But there are dozens of local particular versions which vary like fairy stories retold. The Good Old Days are not quite the same as Merry England, and both are worlds away from the aesthete's conviction of an idyllic past when every workman was an artist-craftsman and could do no wrong. The anonymous heroes of this aesthetic Golden Age are the people who built the village cottages and made the traditional farm tools, and indeed a scythe is astonishingly beautiful with its subtly changing planes. But it does not prove their point. The old craftsmen used natural materials from necessity, and worked them in fixed designs perfected by centuries of use. That their creations please our current sophisticated taste does not mean that they also pleased the taste of their unsophisticated creators. Given the choice, most country people, like most people everywhere, would no doubt always have preferred red plastic to polished ash for the handles of tools. Certainly they prefer it now, and why should we suppose they have changed?

I know that the bricklayer's family have been local craftsmen here for generations; but I also know that his garden harbours a fishing gnome sitting on a rockery where the rocks are lumps of differently coloured concrete. I know that the carpenter's father and grandfather were carpenters before him; but his living-room window is decorated with twin purple vases painted with love-birds, and between them a bowl of plastic daffodils and scarlet roses.

Therefore I also know that the workmen's taste is not ours. It is not that one is good and the other is bad, for how can the virtue of taste be judged except by the pleasure it gives? Simply the bricklayer and the carpenter are happy in one kind of house and we are happy in another, and why should they be aesthetes to suit us? But nonetheless they must never be let choose for us, any more than we for them. The carpenter should keep his much-admired window-sill, but he must let us have our banisters plain.

For the banisters I find installed one Monday are for me an offence which must be removed at whatever cost of hurt feelings: an offence so violent that I protest by reflex action without even time to consider anyone else's feelings but my own. It is the roof-tiles all over again, as the foreman seems to realize, for this time my protest convinces him as quickly and thoroughly as the banisters do me.

"You don't like them?" he asks, dismayed and puzzled.

"No," I say without mitigation. "No." And I tell him exactly what can be done to change them to suit us.

This time he says nothing in reply but only makes notes in his book, and the following Monday the stairs are flanked by banisters simple enough to suit even our uncompromising taste for plainness. If feelings are hurt they are not discussed with me, and if the carpenter is no longer my friend I can't help it. Since I shall not meet him every time I go up and down stairs I shall endure his loss much more easily than his banisters.

But after the first week he seems to bear me no ill-will, for he has never got over his first incredulity that I did not know that staircases are made elsewhere and brought in like pieces of furniture; and I think that for anyone as ignorant of the facts of life as I clearly am, he is ready to make allowances. Obviously I know no better. He is protective rather than resentful.

"You want to mind how you sit about on that grass. It's a cold old wind. You want to wrap up well." We are still friends despite the banisters.

But apart from such incidental readjustments the Mondays pass peacefully, like stages on a journey confidently in sight of its goal. Though whether I am confident or resigned or perhaps only less tired without the Regency Villa, I don't know. Certainly the work is surprisingly more manageable now we stay in London at week-ends. There is more time for everything: not only time on Saturdays and Sundays for the dozens of odd tasks which fit themselves in now unnoticed, but time too in a week relieved of the pressure of the impending weekly transportation.

At the end of autumn the weather is wild again, but we are sheltered now from the gales which drive the falling leaves like flocks of blown birds, and the rain-storms which sweep over the valley to stream down the windows and rattle cheerfully in the water-pipes. The weekly progress is less dramatic now as the work becomes more finicking, but also more convincing as the house approaches its finished state. November. December. Boxing Day is the second Christmas picnic: not on an empty site now but in an almost-finished house. We need a key to let ourselves in, and that in itself is a satisfaction. This time we picnic in style. We walk round the house to decide which room we shall choose. Not the dining-room, for the winter sun shines only slantingly yet in its west-facing window. We shall sit in full sun in the living-room, ignoring the dusty shoes and shiny navy-blue jacket and reels of electric flex dumped in one corner.

The boys are suddenly and surprisingly domestic. They dust the window-sill clean with a dirty sack, bring in two sawing-benches from the room next door for seats, and find a broom for the floor. Stirred by their energetic sweeping, clouds of dust rise like fog from the concrete surface, but I am still so much more house-builder than housekeeper that I am delighted by such convincing proof of dry foundations. We open a window to blow the air clear again, then lay out on the window-sill our elaborate meal of Christmas Day left-overs. We then balance on our narrow benches and eat inordinately.

The low mid-winter sun slants into the room and across to the furthest wall, and even with no heating the temperature is most gratifyingly warmer than out of doors. The house is a glorious success: today we are all convinced. I think it is why the boys have taken over the arrangements. For this meal is not simply a picnic under shelter, it is our first house-warming party. It is very much an occasion, and we drink the house's health in turn, two by two, in wine from the tops of the thermos-flasks.

∞∞∞∞ *27* ∞∞∞∞

Do we want the reeded-glass in the hall door to run upright or horizontal?

Where exactly do we want the electric sockets? Will I please put chalk crosses on the walls?

Have we decided about the banister hand-rails? (Oh those banisters!)

Do we want a brick edging round the flower-bed in that little conservatory bit off the living room?

Do we really want the bedroom doors hung the way they're shown on the plan? Most people have them the other way round to hide the room when they're open.

How many shelves do we want in the airing-cupboard?

Do we want all the curtain-boards fixed to the ceilings, or is it only in the living-room that the curtains are to cover the whole wall?

The builders' merchants *still* haven't replaced that wash-basin they delivered cracked. Will I get on to them again when I go back to London?

Since Banister Monday the foreman's lists of questions have grown steadily longer, and he is no doubt thankful that about the early stages of building a house I was too ignorant to have any opinion. However we are still on good terms: he has invited me to see his garden. And because what the workmen are doing now is entirely within my domestic sphere, the house progresses faster for me than ever before. The plumbers have finished. The electricians are ready for the mains to be connected. There are boards on the bedroom floors where we have balanced so long across the open joists that it is now second-nature never to put down a foot without looking.

Then one Monday the plasterers are here, a pair of furiously busy men who rush about with boards of wet mud and transform the rooms between one week and the next from rough shelters of crudely insistent bricks to spaces defined by peacefully smooth and exactly accurate planes. Of all the stages of a house except the first enclosure of rooms, plastering makes the greatest and most civilizing transformation.

The next week the publishers' furniture is here, built-in cupboards and walls of shelves to the ceilings. The next, all the doors are on and their handles fitted. The weekly questions are now minutely domestic—about the height of draining-boards and the placing of towel-rails, about wardrobe doors and coat-hooks under the stairs, and where should they fix the airer in the bathroom? And, by the way, will I find another set of handles and a letter-box for the front door? The one we chose is out of stock, and we'd better choose for ourselves and not leave it to them or we might not like it. (He still remembers the banisters, but so do I. We will certainly choose.)

At the stage of the coat-hooks and towel-rails a house is so nearly finished that I feel our distant architect should make a special journey south to inspect it before the workmen leave. He arrives one week-end and spends a mysteriously purposeful hour peering into water-tanks and checking floors and woodwork and climbing about the dark roof-space with an electric torch.

"One or two small points, but nothing much that matters. They've made a good job of it." He opens and closes a window experimentally. "Nothing much wrong that I can find." He goes off down the field to look at the septic tank, and I follow for comments. From this lower level the house on its terrace is like a ship: powerful and buoyant, and riding the seas with a triumphant confidence which raises my spirits every time I see it. Even my brother is half-converted to liking.

"Not bad from here, is it, now it's up? It certainly looks better than I expected, I'll give you that. But I can't say I'm really keen. There's nothing to object to about it of course, it's just dull."

But we are quite happy to have it dull. We never set out to build an exciting house to be photographed for my brother's architectural journals.

"It's all right inside though—that I will give you. Wouldn't mind living in it myself. And it's certainly *solid*, which is what you asked for. And well finished-off. You've not done too badly as deputy. You can let me know when you want a job."

This is unnatural brotherly praise, which I never expected. For the main relationship between us, even at our now more-or-less advanced ages, is still the old one of younger brother debunking older sister. The chief difference after twenty years is that exchanges which only amused my brother when I was twenty-one, now at forty-one amuse me as well.

"And you're still alive to live in it—that's the big thing. Heavy losses you know, among hopeful young architects. They're so much given to admiring their own work that they've a habit of standing back on the scaffolding to get a better view of their fine façades, and then they step off the edge and that's that. Nice that you've survived."

"I *don't* much admire the façade, so I daresay that's what's saved me." For I will not rise to his hopeful young architect bait just to please him.

Certainly as wit our exchanges are scarcely on any higher level than the jokes with the workmen, but it is a comfortable long-established relationship between us which survives without effort. And he has finished his inspection now; he makes a final round of the house, leaves me a list for the foreman, then sets off back on his two-hundred-mile journey north.

It is his last visit before the builders leave, an inspection like a medical examination which passes the patient as fit and ready for work. And the following Monday is the day I have waited for as a sign that the house is so nearly finished that I can begin at last to plan for moving in.

"Will you think out what decorations you want," the foreman asks, "and let me know next week?"

As if I had not thought it out months ago! I am surprised that after all this time he knows me no better. But although I have had months for thinking, there is nothing to think about. We want white everywhere I tell him. All the paint certainly, and all the walls, and only some of the ceilings coloured.

"Is that really what you want?" He is touchingly and

ludicrously disappointed, expecting no doubt some exciting colour-schemes in what he calls modern-art style. Clearly from us he was hoping for something extraordinary in the way of decoration: something to describe to the next customers he builds a house for, as he boasts of the previous parquet-flooring to us. But no. White everywhere. And what could be duller?

"It's not at all what I expected," he says. For we seem to him an inexplicable family, and he regards all our doings with hope-ful curiosity. But this time we must disappoint him. I am pre-pared to arrive in my most disreputable country clothes and sit about in wet grass admiring the view; I will pace about the field looking round me at the invisible garden like some poor mad creature escaped from care. If that will do, then I am ready to amuse him, but we will not cover each wall of the living-room with a differently coloured wall-paper as he seems to have hoped we would.

White, I insist. Except for the ceilings we want the house white all through.

"Dead white?" he asks. "Not a nice broken white?"

No, I say firmly. White simply. Dead if he likes to think of it so coldly, but as white anyway as he can make it. For I know very well how quickly white turns to a nice broken white with-out help from anyone. White is a colour of only the very newest paint and distemper, and broken white is what we shall live with willy-nilly after the first pristine months. So the whitest possible white I say firmly, looking at him hard, for I want no Broken-White Crisis to add to Roof-Tile Week and Banister Monday.

When I come out the following Monday the house is trans-formed. It is suddenly clear of all the clutter which has filled it so long. There are no tools, no workmen's jackets on nails, no old shoes, no wood-shavings, no benches, no mugs, no caches of dirt in corners. The rooms are empty and the floors are swept unnaturally clean. The builders have moved out for good and the house is ready for the decorators. In the room nearest the door their gear has replaced the builders'. There are planks and trestles which were not here last week, an assembly of paint tins ranged like the Giants' Causeway, and over the point of the door hang two pairs of clean white overalls.

This is the day when I feel for the first time the house is officially ours. The builders have moved out and our different life has now taken possession. That there is no furniture, no single scrap of anything we have put there makes no difference. The empty rooms have merely been cleared of our things to give the decorators space to work freely: our life surrounds them waiting to settle in again. This for me is the week-end we have moved in; the final departure of the decorators and the furniture arriving from store will be only the outward confirmation of what has already happened. It is today that I can realize our true arrival, not later on in the noise and fuss of furniture vans arriving, and with all the paraphernalia of our domestic lives showered down upon me as if from an exploding aeroplane.

But despite the satisfaction of knowing that this is the final stage before we are settled, there is still a certain regret. This half-finished house has been welcoming and friendly, it has had a cheerful robust personality of rough-brick and clatter, which will vanish with the rest of the intimate ephemeral world on this hill-side. The men and their huts, the tea-bell and the adopted dog—they have gone, and now all the pleasant tissue of this camp-life on the building-site will be lost: the small daily habits and interests, and the well-worn jokes which never ceased to amuse us, and have no more grown stale than the accustomed sunshine since their value was never as intellectual surprises but as a genial climate of goodwill.

I go round the rooms now a little sadly, rooms each with its own definite atmosphere and particular life. One has always been a general store, another is where the men kept their coats and seemed always to feel most at home. There is the living-room with its window-sill picnics, the room the men assigned to me—

long ago it seems now—which has become my familiar and intimate retreat. The middle bedroom has always been the assembly place for discussions, and its window, more than any other in the house, frames the quintessential view of the valley below. But now this communal meeting-place will change to private bedroom. There will be no more rustic-voiced discussions in what is now the kitchen, nor bags of tools in the bottom of wardrobes, nor knapsacks of lunch in cupboards. I shall miss the slow and busy and cheerful life which peopled the house every Monday when I came, and all the rest of the week when I thought about it. Today is the last visit to the house I have inhabited for the last six months.

However it is a mood of the most luxurious regret, an emotional indulgence no more depressing than the regret at leaving our flowery summer garden when we go off on a long-looked-for holiday. As I walk round the rooms I try to register them as they have been till now, so that later on when our different life occupies them I can still remember their first personality. For after today they will change completly. This is a parting visit far more real than leaving the Regency Villa, and I find myself feeling quite absurdly sentimental. For I never expected this— that there would be anything else than jubilation as the day of our moving in drew so markedly nearer. But the builders have made of this roof and walls a different house by their occupation, and their house will be gone forever. Not that they will care, nor even remember: for them it is simply a job like all the other jobs they pass through year after year. But this is the only house we shall ever build, and I am sad to lose any part of its creation.

PART FIVE

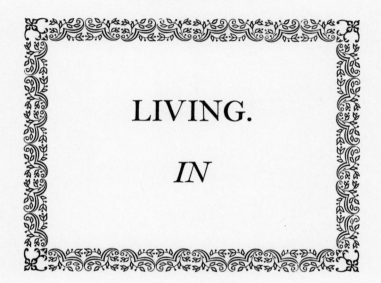

LIVING.

IN

28

MOVING-IN DAY. A MILD GREY MORNING. NO sign of sun, but no sign of rain either, that hazard dreaded above all else by those who move house. The operation has started already. An enormous van has crept cautiously down the drive and edged up close to the house with its tail at the front door. The ramp is already down in position, and inside the van, which is as large as a room, our old familiar furniture is revealed, piled up at ludicrous angles. The driver and his companion have finished admiring the view and are inspecting the house on a heavy-booted perambulation of the bedrooms.

It is odd about removal-men: we meet them only in the domestic crises of our lives when we are at our most distraught and bad-tempered and unreasonable; they see us only at our worst: they can scarcely be expected to like us. Nor is there any reason why *we* should like *them*. They are the instruments of the upheaval which shatters our peace, disrupting the familiar setting of our private lives, and destroying all the intimate comforts and conveniences which develop like the tendrils of a plant when we live long together in any place. There is also the question of our housewifely self-respect. To removal-men are mercilessly revealed all our domestic shortcomings: the chipped cups we pushed to the back of shelves, the chair-seat we stuffed with a cushion instead of mending, the wine-stain on the carpet covered with a rug. Litter behind cupboards, dirt under carpets, cobwebs at the back of pictures—when anyone dismantles a house they must always be astonished at the squalor they have lived in unnoticing. It is not only that a room with the furniture out is a cast-off container which immediately needs redecorating, but even the best of furniture (which ours quite certainly is not) looks shabby and tawdry when wrenched from its context and set out on the pavement or upside-down in a van.

And like our furniture we too are being wrenched from an established life and being set down unceremoniously to make another. When we move house we are awkwardly surrounded by the bits and pieces of living which we must combine to a new organic household life by a kind of energetic domestic shuffling and fidgeting which rearranges the bits and pieces to a comfortable new pattern. Moving house is a dismaying experience for housewives: the worst possible time to make our acquaintance.

Yet the odd thing about removal-men is the goodwill they generate. We might expect to remember them as witnesses of our domestic shame or instruments of our household torture; or if nothing so dramatic, then as unwelcome strangers associated with the general discomfort of moving-house. But not at all: we remember our removal-men as friends, as kind and willing and wonderfully understanding helpers in trouble. They are like doctors called in to perform a domestic operation which we know we must undergo, and we are grateful for their services. And probably over the years of experience with hundreds of distraught housewives, they learn to manage us much as doctors manage patients. Handling the housewife is no doubt a far more important skill in removal-men than handling the furniture.

Not that moving into this house is any kind of trouble. It is neither a domestic crisis, since the family is undisturbed in London, nor a tribulation, since the bad part of the business is breaking up the house we are leaving, and that was long ago accomplished. Today is no more than unpacking our things from store and arranging them at leisure in newly decorated rooms. Today is entirely pleasure, a form of high luxury masquerading as work.

Besides, these removal-men are my long-standing friends and I am always delighted to see them. For as a country firm they are not limited to house-moving; they also sell coal and sand and gravel and manure and top-soil: anything likely or unlikely that their lorries can carry. All through the war they delivered the meagre coal-ration to our farmhouse, with now and then a bag of new sand for the children's sand-pit. It was these same two men who removed us to London, that truly dramatic transplanting of our family life from country to metropolis. And despite the tribulations which followed, I still remember the removal-day with pleasure, an exhilarating holiday jaunt of travelling to London in the van with the furniture, sitting in an easy chair the men arranged for me at the back with a view out over the tail-board.

In the settled years since then our contact has been mostly an enthusiastic waving as van passed car on the local country roads, but we met at the Regency Villa from time to time when they brought us yards of gravel for the paths, and now and then I would call at their office to leave an order and stay to gossip.

"Well now, my dear." It is Percy the older brother of the firm deciding it is time we settled down to the work of the day. He produces a kitchen chair from the van and puts it beside the door.

"You just sit yourself down there, my dear, and don't you never stir, and as we bring in each load you just tell us exactly where you want it put."

But he is not yet quite satisfied about my comfort. He climbs up into the front of the van and reaches for a decrepit cushion which he shakes up, dusts, puts on the chair, and pats invitingly.

"You just sit yourself there, my dear, and make yourself easy. No need for you to lift a finger—that's what we're here for. What's more, you'll save us a mort of trouble if you'll just sit still and tell us where we're to put stuff."

I sit as I'm told and the unloading starts. That desk in the study. That old easy chair in the middle bedroom. The sewing-machine in the living-room cupboard. And the children's old toy-box of hundreds of coloured bricks? Yes. Where? In the conservatory for the moment until I decide.

I keep to my chair with an effort and direct the loads. The slatted teak garden table in the living-room, and that white-painted desk is really a dressing-table—the mirror's somewhere—and that bench goes in the bathroom. And the glass cases of stuffed birds I bought in a sale once and can't bear to part with? I look at them doubtfully: they are much larger than I remembered. There is a pair of pintail-ducks standing among rushes, a family group of two shell-ducks with four young ducklings, and an even more enormous case of snowy-white gulls suspended airily against a pale-blue sky. They make an impressive display in the doorway and we all admire them.

"You don't see nothing like that there done today do you? Wonderful workmanship. You'd reckon they was alive if you knew no different. As good as Madame Tussaud's they are." Yes. But where shall we put them? The conservatory again I suppose. I can see already that what I meant to be a leafy extension to the living-room will simply be a ground-floor attic unless I find somewhere else for our precious white elephants.

Half an hour. An hour. The unloading goes peacefully on, for the two men radiate an unhurrying confidence which banishes fuss. However I doubt whether I am naturally a sitter still, and in any case how can I stay fixed to a chair for hours in a doorway when the rooms behind me are filling up with furniture I long to arrange and find how it fits? But I can see how frustrating it is to stand with a load and not know where to put

it, and I watch for a chance, with both men safely routed, to slip
off on quick inspections. Not that they hesitate to call me if they
notice the empty chair. They have a special hooting summons
which brings me hurrying back like a guilty dog.

I sit and watch them enviously as they lift and carry without
effort weights I could barely move. It is partly a matter of use
and of muscle power, but not entirely. It is also a matter of levers.
For watching them I realize that my own arms and legs are quite
simply too long to be efficient. If we are to use ourselves as
levers for lifting we need to be short and powerful, as these men
are and I am not. I am fundamentally the wrong shape, I am
inches taller than they are and inches narrower, and however
long I practise I shall never walk effortlessly upstairs with a chair
in one hand and a table in the other.

Which is all the more reason for sitting still and directing, as
they have by now several times pointed out in rebuke of my
empty chair. And as they pass me in and out we carry on frag-
mented conversations. The driver breeds tropical fish: they are
not so much his hobby as his chief preoccupation. He shows
them in competitions all over the country and wins prizes from
serious judges. I know all about them and ask the right questions
as he passes my chair.

"Yes," he says proudly. "Last week in London. Two seconds
and a third. (This divan in the little bedroom?)" Then on the
way down again empty-handed—"What's always my worry is
electricity black-outs. (Hand me them drawers out, will you
Percy?) Fish needs a steady temperature to survive. (Upstairs or
down?) And they must have air pumped through constant."
(The drawers are upstairs now and he is down again.) "More to
it than you'd think, you know, rearing fish."

Percy is the one who calls me "my dear," a man about sixty,
of the suitable strong square shape for lifting, and white-haired
(I should guess from his eyebrows) beneath the cap which he
never takes off. Whatever the season he is always dressed in the

same way whenever I see him—in a large pair of trousers held up under his arm-pits by braces, a spotlessly clean white shirt with rolled-up sleeves and a collarless neckband neatly fastened with a stud—and his cap. The cap is not simply a head decoration he puts on and off according to custom, it is something he wears as an essential part of his clothes.

In the course of unpacking they have come on the kettle and teapot and greet them with delight. They put on the water to boil while I fetch the tea and milk and sugar I remembered to bring with me from London. Officially released from my chair at last by the ritual of tea-making, I find they have furnished the kitchen without any instructions from me. The table is in place with the chairs arranged round it, there are cups in the dresser and spoons in the drawer. I give them the tea to make as they like it, and it comes out as black as treacle; but this time, being almost equally guest and hostess, I can water mine down without offence.

"Yes. I remember when all the removing was done with horses." Percy settles down to peaceful reminiscing over his teacup, and his statement is not a non sequitur but a continuation of what he was telling me the last time we met. I suppose he must associate different topics with different housewives just as he associates the furniture, and the years which have passed since our last removal are no more to him than an extended pause in the conversation.

"Yes. A hard day's journey it was from here to London—even with a good team of horses. Yes. And the hills. Knew every inch of London—had to—by the hills. Some slopes so steep you couldn't get up. Not with a full load you couldn't. Had to go miles round sometimes. And the furniture too. Not this light, easy stuff you have nowadays. Real solid pieces—solid mahogany mostly. Ever tried carrying a six-foot mahogany sideboard?"

Percy finishes his tea with relish and I pour him another cup.

"No sugar for me, my dear, thank you. Slimming. That's what I am—slimming. Lost a stone since last back-end and feel no end the better for it. No end better. Yes. I'd begun to put on weight proper. Got altogether too much of a good thing. Couldn't see me feet for me belly. Blown I was—even just walking upstairs. I'd got that fat I reckon I could of rolled as easy as walk." He sips his sugarless tea. "But I'm going down nicely now." It is as if he felt himself to be a balloon deflating. "Yes, a stone since last back-end." And he pulls out the loose waist of his trousers to show me the gap once filled by his now vanished belly.

I should be delighted to sit and hear about horse-van removals and Percy's figure for the rest of the morning, but the fish-fancier has no doubt heard it all before and is far more interested in our kitchen.

"What's that then?"

"That" is a picture propped up on the dresser, a large Dufy print of a light-hearted summery blue and green smudge of trees and water. It is the very essence of summer holiday evoked by paint, and this the men feel as cheerfully as I do; it is only the style which bothers them.

"I reckon that's what they call Modern Art."

"Yes. It's an art on its own I should say."

"Mad isn't it?" (There is no hint of scorn; it is a statement simply.)

"Yes. But what does it represent would you say?"

"I reckon it's meant to be bathing and boating. You can see. That's meant for a boat—badly drawn I grant you—but I reckon that's what it's meant to be—a rowing-boat. Look, there's the oars."

"No. I reckon it's a picture of a nudist camp. Just look at that." (A nudge and a chuckle.) "And that one's sitting and watching. Don't blame him neither."

"Yes. I daresay you've got it. That's it. Bathing and boating in a nudist camp. Enjoying the sunshine. Does you good—don't it?—to see them all happy." Percy beams big-hearted approval. "Wouldn't mind joining them meself for that matter."

He sounds surprised at his own daring, as well he might, for a man who is embarrassed even to take off his cap is no natural joiner of nudist camps.

"Well what about it mate? We'd better get going again. We don't want to be late finishing. We're behindhand this week as it is," he explains to me. "I took the day off yesterday with the wife and it's set us back proper. I didn't ought to of went of course, but I couldn't seem to get out it. You ladies always gets your own way." (He winks at me and chuckles.) "Well, what about it?" (He gets up and hitches his trousers.) "We'd better get going again. Thanks for the tea, my dear. Just what we needed."

By lunch-time the van is empty, but there is still another load to come. "Weren't worth packing it close for such a short ride. Simpler to make two journeys. So we'll be off home now for us dinners, and be back soon after with the rest of the stuff. We'll have you all settled and shipshape by tea-time you'll see."

As indeed they do, even to the sheets in the linen-cupboard and the reading-lamps by the beds, and the books unpacked and arranged on the shelves in unlikely juxtaposition.

"Now you just take a look round by yourself, my dear, while we drink our teas. And see if you can't find any more jobs for us before we leave you. That's what we're here for, you know. No sense in you struggling with things by yourself when we're gone. You've only to say. We'll move the whole lot round if you want. (He beams at me with a generous smile.) We know what you ladies are. Never satisfied till you've tried out every blame thing in half-a-dozen different places. My wife's just the same, my dear, so I know all about it. You don't have to tell me."

Who can wonder that we love our removal-men?

◇◈◇◈◇ *29* ◈◇◈◇◈

But he is wrong: there is nothing to move. For my long-ago planning of the rooms by mat-sizes began by arranging the necessary furniture and the circulation round it, and with so much wall-space taken up already by windows and cupboards and wardrobes and bookshelves there is little choice left about where to put the remaining movables. I walk round the house to see how the men have arranged it, and except for nudging a sofa or table a few inches one way or the other, there is nothing to move. All the dispositions are so simple and so inevitable that no one who lived in these rooms would ever be likely to arrange them very differently.

The men have gone now, waving cheerful farewells and tooting their horn as they drive away down the lane. The house is ours at last. We are in. It is the longed-for culmination of two years' effort: we are safely installed in a house which two years ago was a mere perfectionist's fancy. Here it is, solidly achieved.

I walk slowly through from room to welcoming room, for even on this grey evening of late winter the house is friendly. And despite its informal ease it has an air of serenity—of dignity, if it did not sound so pretentious a word for this comfortably shabby domestic setting. It is not large but it is simple and spacious, and the landscape is part of the house as we hoped it would be, so that even now that the furniture and carpets have made an indoor setting, we shall still live in the country. This house will indeed be our snail-shell, enclosing and sheltering our physical lives without containing our consciousness. We could live here in a space only large enough to hold a bed and yet suffer no sense of being shut in.

Certainly a great many comfortable people would thoroughly dislike so unsnug an arrangement. But a liking for living in cottages is not one William and I share with the cottage-loving English. Certainly they are charming from the outside, but in their dolls'-house interiors we stifle and long for space. Not so much physical as mental space: we grow uneasy to feel our lives enclosed in their cosily confining walls, with the whole outside world reduced to a glimpse of pink roses between muslin curtains. We would rather be cold than cramped, and until we can afford central-heating we will simply wear warm clothes indoors as well as out.

To me the house seems beautiful, and our shabby old furniture is utterly unworthy of its setting. For our things are an odd assortment collected during the war years at local country sales, and mostly bought for the standard bid of ten shillings for a cupboard or chest-of-drawers and fifteen shillings for a table or dresser. Only a glass-fronted bookcase (our kitchen-cupboard) cost more than a pound, and an enormous side-board with drawers each side of a central space; with the door taken off to leave a knee-hole for sitting it is much the best desk we have ever had. Everything is solid and comfortable, and now pleasantly homogeneous since any original differences were long ago hidden under layers of white paint. And right from the start the rooms are cheerfully shabby, with the familiar domestic shabbiness most houses only achieve by long living-in: it is like wearing our favourite old clothes on holiday. Even the furniture seems at home, for every chair and table and chest-of-drawers has a comfortable air of being where it is, not by anyone's arbitrary decision, but from settling down in the exactly right position achieved through years of domestic shuffling about.

I remember someone once telling me sadly that his wife kept their house so immaculate and so exactly in the current fashion that when they died no one would know they had lived there. And I grieved with him for such a chilly and anonymous domesticity, like living all one's life in smart hotels. But unfashionable, so very far from immaculate that the word would never occur to anyone, this house is certainly *ours*. It is unmistakably the mould of our peculiar and individually various way of living, and anyone who knows us would recognize it as ours, even if we all four scattered at the round earth's imagined corners.

Of course this elegant new house is worthy of better things than our ten-shilling oddments in a setting of universal white-wash. We designed the house with a great deal of care, and the decorating and furnishing now need the same attention. It is like an excellent suitcase carelessly stuffed with shabby old clothes, and one day I will repack it suitably with a carefully chosen country wardrobe. But not now. The house itself has been an effort of domestic nest-egg-laying which has exhausted for the time being the very last flicker of my interest in house-making. We are in. The rest can wait for my enthusiasm to revive again. The house as it is will do us perfectly well, and what matters in the next few years is the garden.

But the garden too must wait for the moment. We are in now, but still only awkwardly in. For though the furniture may be comfortable, we certainly shall not be unless I busy myself before the others arrive, and arrange in more domestic detail.

It is mid-week: William and the boys will be here at the week-end. If the house is to be ready for them on Friday night I must work every waking hour of the two days between—making up beds, allocating cupboards, wiring up electric fires and bed-side reading-lamps, arranging all the paraphernalia of living—the pots and pans and tools in places where we shall all know where to find them without asking. I put food in the pantry and daffodils in the living-room and hot-water bottles in the beds. It is Friday evening: I am ready to welcome them. I even change into tidier clothes before they come, for this is a ceremonial occasion, the culminating moment of more than two years' effort.

It is also a great surprise.

Certainly I know my family better than to expect an emotional demonstration, but still I did expect some kind of reaction to this transplanting of their week-end lives to a brand-new setting. No culminating moment perhaps, but certainly a pleased astonishment to find themselves rehoused so very pleasantly.

But not at all. They arrive. They survey. They take possession. It is an occupation as swift as Caesar's. In the first hour they are all three as completely at home as if they had lived here already for years and had only moved out for a few weeks' absence.

Am I disappointed? Yes. A little. But surprised more than anything else. Though really I should know better after years of living with their confident taking-for-granted of all domestic arrangements. For they seem to feel that households run of their own accord like rivers, that comfortable settings for living-in arrange themselves without human effort. But I daresay their confidence is the truest compliment that could be paid to any house, and certainly this one suits us so perfectly that from the first day we know we are home. The conviction that we have lived here already for years astonishes us all and not only me. It is like a love-affair when at first meeting each feels they have known the other for all of their lives that matters.

The week-ends that follow confirm the family's unconscious praise, for all the domestic organization of living arranges itself with a frictionless inevitability. Like shoes made to measure the house fits us perfectly from the start: there is no uncomfortable period of breaking each other in and adjusting ourselves to the house or the house to us. We planned the house to suit us, and now it takes over our domestic life with scarcely any conscious attention from us, leaving us free for our other more interesting concerns. I have never been in a house where the mere business of living needed so little time and attention.

Which is just as well, for there is little time and less attention. This summer I must spend on the garden not the house.

Living. *In*

Not on gardening as generally understood—nothing to do with growing plants—but clearing up the derelict area of maltreated field which surrounds the house on every side. It must be tidied and raked and levelled before any thought of making a garden, and I already foresee the summer ahead as a season of hard labour. And labour mostly my own, for the others are not interested in gardens, and why after all should they spend their weekends toiling on a patch of field simply because that is how I choose to spend mine?

It is not that I enjoy it any more than they would. Not at all. But I want a garden, and if I am to have one then this is how the operation must begin. And however dull this first stage may be in itself, it is still just tolerable as the start of the way to the green and flowery conclusion. So I labour: week-end after week-end without making any noticeable difference to so large an area of ground.

The spring passes, and the beech-woods grow dark on the hills. The summer flows over us in weeks of fine weather, a blue summer of settled sunshine. It is Dunkirk weather, so we would once have told ourselves, but in the years of uneasy peace we have forgotten that this holiday weather is when our enemies are most active against us, and wars grow as rankly as weeds. May is over now, and June nearly gone, with wild roses and elder-blossom in the hedges, and the country lying warm and quiet through the summer solstice.

Every week-end now is as long as we can make it. We travel out early on Friday evenings to have an extra summer night in the country and Saturday as a long unbroken day. And on Sundays our friends come out from London to see our new house, arriving in numbers which overflow the dining-table into deck-chairs on the terrace. Friends invited for lunch and staying on for tea and supper, as I know they will, and make sure of food enough for their astonishing, uninhibited, day-in-the-country appetites.

It is high summer now, and with Midsummer Day already
behind us the season will soon begin to change imperceptibly to
middle-age and autumn. In the field across the valley they have
already come to mow the hay which has followed last year's
corn, a ley underplanted perhaps to grow through the stubble.
We have watched it all summer, flowing in the wind like water
and running with currents of swaying movement across the
meadow-surface. It is like seeing the wind made visible and
watching it move in dapples across the grass like cat's-paws
across water.

But now they have come to cut it. The scarlet tractor roars
round the field, and as its invisible blades move low throughout
the stalks, the grass falls in long swathes lying all one way like
swiftly flowing streams. It lies very flat on the level field and the
grass-stalks shine in the sun, fallen in the plaited patterns of
moving water, like the hair of da Vinci's women. It is as if the
field were covered all over with parallel streams, and this green
self-striping of the swathes is speckled with dark birds eating the
grass-seed. Above the flat rows they stand unnaturally large,
bold and bouncing over the grass, stretching up their necks to
look around them: the very incarnation for me of country mid-
summers.

A week away in London and the next week-end our hay is
tossed to dry, and the sleekly shining hair of new grass is tedded
to a frowzy uncombed frizz. It is tossed again in this drying
weather, is baled and carried, and now the field is bare and
awkward like a newly shorn sheep.

> "The first load of hay
> Drives the cuckoo away."

The farmer's hay is loaded and the cuckoos have stammered
and gone. But the glow-worms are here: dozens and dozens of
them all about the garden, shining unearthly green among the
grass-stalks. I never expected glow-worms this year after the

builders' trampling, but perhaps by day they are not vulnerable grubs in the grass waiting to be trodden on, but hide themselves away somewhere safe. Certainly there are more this year than ever before, everywhere along the sides of the drive and the edges of the long grass, transforming the leafless garden to a setting for *A Midsummer Night's Dream.*

And this glow-worm dark is the only time the garden does not depress me, for by day it is quite simply a barren area of broken-up ground which I labour to bring into order. And labour, not perhaps unavailingly, but with progress so slow it is scarcely noticeable from one week to the next.

But there are impressive compensations. The surrounding country for one (I can lift mine eyes to the hills and ignore the garden), and the house unfailingly. When the world is too much with me in the shape of uncultivated wilderness, then I shut myself up and recover in its haven: in the comforting, the peaceful, the civilized, the leisured, the beautiful, the much-loved, the already-achieved, and entirely satisfactory house.

This house is much more than the shelter of walls we live in, and built anywhere else than here it would be a different house entirely. For more essential than even its walls is the landscape in the windows, the deliberately imposed consciousness of the countryside it is set in. This house now defines this valley for everyone who comes here, and the landscape radiates from its fixed focus as the world for each of us radiates from our own individual consciousness. The siting of the building and placing of the windows will from now on impose on the mind of every-one who lives here a particular conception of the surrounding country. Of all the varying visual interpretations of this valley, from higher or lower on the slope, or from different directions along the hill-side, this is the exact version which will now exist in hundreds of human minds: this exact slope of the land, and line of the hills, and interaction of the different planes of the landscape one against the other.

It is as if from the changing flow of the country scene this particular arrangement had been defined and given permanent reality. It is fixed now and accessible. The house has *created* the view. The valley was always here, but the valley is not the view. The valley is an indifferent area of the earth's surface, a minor depression in the chalk, covered with the vegetation of a temperate climate. The valley's existence is independent of human beings: it is part of the non-human world they temporarily inhabit. But the view is human: the view is the valley consciously registered by human eyes and mind.

"These things were here and but the beholder wanting." So Hopkins says of a different scene. And now this house is the beholder. From these things which were here—from the inhuman elements of space and hills and trees—the house has created a human countryside, and the alien natural world of this valley is linked to our human lives by a house which is conscious of both.

◇◇◇◇ *30* ◇◇◇◇

The end of July and the start of school holidays. Since William is travelling abroad for most of August the boys and I will spend the absent time in the country; and if I will have their friends to stay, then they will help me in the garden. It is their idea of barter, not mine, for I have always considered the succession of visiting friends as part of the essential housekeeping. But this first summer is no time for altruism, and I eagerly accept their bargain.

The three of us settle ourselves in with the greatest satisfaction to our usual way of holiday life in the country: a careless camping-out style of existence which the boys and I relapse to immediately when left alone. Living has no routine of any kind, simply the hours run into days, the days into weeks in an uninterrupted stream of doing as we like. We keep no hours either clock or daylight, but go to bed and get up as we fancy or as sleep overtakes us. There are no set meals, we simply stop for food when hunger reminds us, calling the others to come and join us. And the meals themselves are reduced to the lowest simplicity of what can be eaten as it is or as it comes out of tins. By our camping-out standards the plainest dishes are elaborate cookery: porridge made deliberately lumpy (for we have our particular perversions), beans on toast, eggs and bacon—these rank as high-holiday cuisine. Fortunately boys have grateful appetites, and though far from indiscriminate as people suppose, their prejudices are against rather than for the niceties of cooking. As for me, I care no more than they do in this carefree season. Any meal which can be prepared and eaten in half an hour is for me a holiday favourite. It is wonderfully simple. When the sink fills with pots we wash them all up together in a single clean sweep, and when the pantry is empty we all go down to the village together and stock up again with what we each fancy.

There is no housework, no cleaning, no bother with clothes. We spend the day out of doors in the sun, and when the evening grows cool we come in again to the sun-warmed house. It is the business of living reduced to its simplest essentials, and on summer holiday there seems no reason why it should ever change or come to an end. We are uninterruptedly content.

Best of all are the early mornings (*my* early mornings, for boys of this age are inveterate sleepers-in), cool and dewy now after the clear August nights. But the angle of the terrace is warm already, warm enough to sit and plan the sunshiny day ahead before I finish my coffee and walk round the garden. The garden? Well, what other name if not garden? Anyway I walk round. And coming back this morning along the hedge by the road I stop suddenly short at a trail of white through the grass. It is the path where I once saw the fox, a narrow track of short turf threading through the long grass and tunnelling out of sight under the brambles and through the hedge, a usually secret path now made glaringly obvious by a stripe of white on either side. It is as if a white-wash brush had swept along the bordering grass-stalks to mark out the way under the hedge. The white tunnel disappears in green shadow, but surely I can find it again where it crosses the road. I go round by the gate. Yes. There it is. Through the opposite hedge, up the bank and on up the hill-side. Grass-stalks, leaves, low branches, twigs—the white-wash trail is easy to follow, it is only the close-grown tangle of briars and willow-herb which hinders me. Steadily on up-hill (the slope is surprisingly steep), covering my face with my hands as I push through thorny thickets, and here at last is what I have come to find: a large dark hole plunging into the hill, and at the entrance an enormous pile of chalk-white rubble and broken rock brought up from deep in the hill-side. It is a newly dug badger sett.

Of all the places badgers like to live, this valley is exactly right, so the Forestry man told us. A wooded hill-side facing south on well-drained soil. They like the edges of woods he says, with a sheltering slope behind and open country below. (But badgers are not the only ones to like it: there is nothing more satisfactory.)

From the pile of rubble I choose a piece of chalk scored by deep claw-marks as evidence, and go back to tell the boys of my find. They are humped in their beds still, drowned in sleep, their consciousness deep below layers of oblivion. I rock them gently by the shoulders to bring them to the surface, and announce the news to their sleeping ears. But I can never really bring myself to rock hard enough to rouse them, restrained always by remorse at depriving anyone of the sleep which for me is so hard to come by.

Living. *In*

Nothing happens. I rock them again and repeat the news—that I've found a badger sett. Newly dug. And a path to it through the garden. Do they want me to show them?

Still nothing happens. If their ears have taken in the information it has not yet sunk down to their consciousness. It is a slow process which has not yet had time to produce results. But it will. I leave them and go down to put on the kettle for breakfast.

"What did you say just now?" It is a sleepy voice over the banisters "Did you say something about badgers?"

They pull on their clothes as they come downstairs. Breakfast must wait. We go back up the hill. A cavern of a hole and a pile of chalk like a coal-tip and the boys are most gratifyingly impressed. But what they want to see now, they say, are the badgers. Do they only come out at night? How late at night? In this season of hungry young might they come out early, while there is still enough twilight to see them?

We are now three would-be badger-watchers and there is nothing in the world we want to see more than a striped snout nosing through our hedge. We wait for a warm and windy night: warm for our comfort, windy to scatter our scent. Or so we hope. At dusk we settle ourselves downwind of the leafy tunnel where the chalk-whitened track comes through the hedge. We all sit a little apart from each other, separated by the high grass waving between us. At this sitting height the swaying grass-heads move at eye-level: it is as if we were in boats on a flowing sea, and beyond the soft waves which surround us the darkening valley is the solid land, a just-visible pattern of grey fields outlined by black hedges.

In the hedge behind us the trees are in summer leaf, not folding against each other soft and noiseless as they did in spring, but firm now like stiff paper, rustling together in a swaying rhythm like the heave of waves rising and falling. And faintly in the lulls, like the sound of the sea a long way off, is a soft background murmuring from all the hundreds of trees on the hill behind us.

The wind smells of hay and honey, and we sit apart and very still in the rocking grass, looking out over the valley now almost lost in the growing darkness. The hedge beside us shows only in outline now, darker shapes of trees moving against the sky, the hedge-maples bunchy, ash-leaves like fern-fronds, and the pliant young beech twigs streaming wet feathers in the wind. Against the black hedge the flat white flowers of the hog-weed sway like pale saucers. The boys sit motionless each side of me in their nests of grass and I wonder what they are thinking.

From being so long silent and still we have lost our human identity, and the night flows over us like water over the drowned. We are less real than the wind or the swaying trees or even the unseen badgers: we no longer exist except as creatures experiencing the night—half-nervous creatures in this unknown element, and I think if a badger's striped head appeared from the hedge beside us we should tense with alarm as much as excitement.

But no head does appear. There is nothing moving except moths flying swift and erratic through the warm darkness, and the wind which is the night enveloping us. In any case what would badgers find to eat, I wonder, in this meadow cropped short by the cows? Mice perhaps (do they eat mice?) or beetles, or perhaps the large black slugs which come out at dusk. Enormous slugs. As big as crocodiles. So huge we need a gun to shoot them. And by the end of the summer, if they go on growing, we shall have to go out in pairs together for protection.

We begin to fidget. If a badger came now it is too dark to see it. Which is no doubt one of the many drawbacks of badger-watching. The boys are bored, they fidget unmistakably, and before this reassertion of their identity the night recedes. They signal across the waving grass and converse in dumb-show. They are hungry (one pats his hollow-sounding stomach) and cold (the other chatters his teeth dramatically). Let's give up badgers and go indoors (they get up and take me silently each by a hand and pull me to my feet). We stretch and shake ourselves and shiver (we are colder than we thought sitting so long in moist grass) and make for the house. We are disillusioned: our badger-watching days are over.

But badgers, even these unsatisfactory invisible specimens, are light entertainment in this holiday which for me is mostly work. The garden is the worst, is unremitting labour, even though the boys help as they promised and have taken over the grass-cutting entirely; a valiant task considering the area of field enclosed for garden. But the house too needs time spent on it, for though we live content in our careless comfort, much is still make-shift. Curtains are too short or too long, chairs need recovering and carpets rebinding, the desk doesn't fit in the study, and all the white-painted furniture needs repainting now it is no longer half-hidden in shadowy rooms but basks on the sunny walls of our new white house.

But none of it matters. It is all done for pleasure, a strenuous form of pleasure perhaps, but not more than tennis-playing or mountain-climbing or all the other hard-working occupations human beings undertake for enjoyment. I wake early and lie in bed and look out at the shining blue sky in the window and think of Dr. Johnson's strawberry. There may be a greater pleasure than a house in the country, but if so I can't imagine it these fine summer mornings. Nor is it a simple pleasure, although it might seem so at first glance. On the contrary it is very complicated. And unlike the simpler biologically arranged pleasures like sex or food, it needs a long background preparation of steady interest to emerge as pleasure at all. This is not the Simple Life. About that I have no illusions. It is a life of extreme privilege. I may wear disreputable old clothes, live on Boy Scout food, fall into bed at night sunburnt and aching with tiredness from twelve hours gardening in the sun—but still it is a life of privilege. Leisure, health, a standard of living high enough to let me be preoccupied with the unproductive labour of making a garden: these are the underlying essentials of this seeming-simple life. It is much like Marie-Antoinette's dairy-farming. For the fact that I exhaust myself working like a labourer is nothing to do with the case. It is what I choose to do, and what millions and millions of other town-dwellers would choose if they could. I am privileged and I am grateful, and the faintly smug feeling as I lie in bed and look at the sky, that I have after all done a great deal of work to earn so privileged a state, only makes the state more thoroughly satisfactory.

◇◇◇◇◇ 31 ◇◇◇◇◇

Somewhere there is a quotation I only half-remember about civilization reaching Bear Island when Horace Walpole (could it be?) passed by on some northern cruise. Certainly that is how I feel now about William and this house, for the boys are away with friends at the sea, William and and I have the house to ourselves, and life blossoms at last into leisure.

The early September weather holds high and blue, day after day the mellowing sun floods dawn through the hazy air, and in the early mists of the windless mornings the landscape emerges a layer at a time like a Chinese painting. And in this civilizing season there is suddenly time to be civilized, hour after unhurried hour simply for enjoying.

It is leisure created by William, for I use up time like a raw material in what I am making, but William creates it. He uses the day as a framework for living in, and his day has more hours than mine because he is conscious of them, as I seldom am of the hours consumed by the business of doing. The livers and the doers: perhaps it is nearer than users and makers. But whatever we call ourselves we cannot choose which we are, but can only experience the other rôle vicariously through a different personality.

As I now do through William. The whole climate of living has changed. The day I wake to now is no longer so many working hours before dark, but is an occasion, an informal ceremony of leisure. We get up at the proper time now, not haphazard as I do when left alone, waking at all hours of dark or daylight. We sit at ease on the terrace and drink our breakfast coffee, and this morning the view in front of us is subtly different because of the day ahead. The gentle hollow of the valley lies below us, and as always when the light is sideways there is this sense of floating. We are weightless: we have only to commit ourselves to the willing air to plane out over the smiling meadows as effortlessly as the kestrel sweeping over our heads from the hill behind us. It is this hollow space of the valley which gives the view depth and resonance, which makes it vivid as other scenery only is in certain lights or in the rain-washed air between thunder-storms.

Wide views are strangely consoling—it is what William feels here always—consoling and calming. As if our troubled human state were comforted by even the fleeting experience of their absolute serenity.

There are sheep in the field below ours, uneasy creatures never properly domesticated. Cows settle down at home in their fields, but not sheep. They wander about, are curious, explore the hedges, try to get out. And even as sheep go, these are a restless lot. I watch them from bed in the mornings, and can tell by their behaviour exactly what is happening out of sight behind us on the other side of the house. For they take an unfailing interest in our affairs, and stop their eating to watch every caller who comes down the drive. At the postman on his bicycle they placidly stare, the newspaper van makes them vaguely uneasy, the railway lorry definitely upsets them; but when the next-door dog comes through the hedge they all flock together in alarm and stamp their silly feet.

But I like to have them near, for the mournful cry of sheep in the wind is part of my childhood. I have only to shut my eyes to feel the North-country hills all round me and smell the high moorland mist. Even these rump-fed runions of the south can haunt the wind with nostalgia. They are watching the gate now and moving a few steps forwards. The morning papers have come.

To walk round the garden with William is for me a curious experience, for I cease to be a gardener. Our walk is a short stroll together to savour the open air, and the lane would do equally well as a setting. When I walk round the garden alone I am part-inspector, part-planner and wholly concerned with the garden. But gardeners are tiresome companions for non-gardeners, are restless and preoccupied, and when I walk with William I cease to register the garden. We stroll and converse and I feel like Bear Island visited.

The mornings are mildly busy, with a desultory form of housekeeping wonderfully restful after the working weeks. I tidy the house and change the flowers, I shop in the village and cook a lunch which has nothing to do with tins of beans or porridge and treacle. Even in the morning I sit in a deck-chair and read, and wonder how anyone can sit with a book at mid-morning without feeling guilty. But guilty or not, I read and sit. Not gardening books either, but the neglected newspapers I seldom read when alone, and Clare's poetry, which does so well in the country, and Dostoevsky, who doesn't. For I realize it is time to lay aside *Crime and Punishment* when I find myself thinking how badly Raskolnikov would drive a car.

This is the first time we have lived in the house as it was meant for living, and because for William listening to music is a satisfaction which grows steadily more profound, all the week the house breathes music like a fragrance. The early composers who are William's favourites fill the hollow shell of walls with melodious constructions of sound, and radiate sweet order through the open windows. And of them all Purcell is most at home in this green English valley, his music as natural as bird-song.

In the afternoons we walk. We follow the footpaths which criss-cross the countryside, and for the first time since we came to this valley I explore the hills and woods which surround us. The landscape I have lived with all this time as a view from the house is translated now into real three-dimensional country. It is no longer simply something I look at, but a place which contains us: where I know the slopes by climbing them, not merely as curves in a picture; and the woods not as dark shapes in the landscape but as trees which meet over my head. And the view is changed. I know now what the valley looks like from the other side, from the top of the hill, from half-a-mile along the lane— and now all these different versions are implied in the valley framed in the windows. Our own particular view is still the theme, but developed now by remembered variations.

On all the miles of the PUBLIC FOOTPATHS we are the only walkers. Only now and again we pass files of little girls on ponies: always girls and always of much the same age, which is just before puberty. Do little boys never ride horses I wonder? Certainly they don't ride them here. The clip-clop past along the lane is always troops of moppets, and I think the corresponding phase in small boys is to want to be farmers. However not farmers who do dull things like growing corn, but farmers who keep cows and pigs and horses more or less as pets, so perhaps after all there is not so much difference between the sexes. But still it seems odd that galloping about on a horse's back should not be a fine manly sport, but only the next stage on for girls too old for dolls and too young for boy-friends.

They are very polite little girls and thank us prettily when we stand aside to let them pass. And we are delighted to meet them, not for any reason that they would suppose, but because it is only the trampling of their ponies' hooves that keeps the footpaths open through the brambles and willow-herb and wild raspberries which steadily overgrow them now no one goes country-walking except an odd couple out from London for a week of September holiday.

For we see more of the local animals than the local people, not only sheep and cows but our neighbouring fox, which comes through the hedge by the badgers' path and crosses the garden with one eye on our windows. And as always in open country with larks, there are hares, huge jack-knifing hares that lollop across the meadows and will no doubt lollop into the garden and eat our young trees when we plant them. Birds too, for now William has calmed the gales of my usual preoccupations, I notice how unconcerned the birds are by our accepted presence. Not only garden birds, the tits and robins and blackbirds and thrushes and starlings and linnets, but even the wary magpies bounce over the garden grass, and buccaneering jays swoop down from the hedge to take the bread I throw through the window, setting off all the accustomed sparrows in a fuss and twitter of domestic alarm.

In such tranquil occupations we spend the days of blue September weather, quiet days with double the time of any I spend alone. Then one morning we wake to wind and the calm weather is over, and since wind destroys the texture of the day, the hour is without identity. For in fine still weather, early morning has an atmospheric pattern, and we can tell by a dozen niceties, without need of watches, just how far the day has progressed: by the quality of the light and the birdsong, and the chill or warmth of the dewy landscape. But wind scatters all. No grey dew which might be frost, no growing warmth as the sun contracts the shadows, but simply a universal turbulence of air which gives the whole day a sameness, all the delicate progression of a fine September morning stirred by the wind to a kind of atmospheric soup.

In this house which is half windows and the windows half sky we live very close to the weather, the various, subtle, ever-changing, mercurial weather which is England's greatest beauty. It is like Cleopatra, and custom never stales its infinite variety. Our weather is island weather fresh and changeable, the soft air moist and the sky patterned with clouds. We are always conscious that the sea is near, and over any range of English hills we can always imagine a watery horizon.

But sometimes, when the wind blows from the east, we lose our island climate and share with Europe its continental summer: bright and hot and rainless. At first we delight in the sun, the reliable sun blazing gloriously down from a cloudless sky. Blazing day after day (we begin to be bored), week after week (is there any reason why it should ever change?), blazing always the same in the same empty sky (would it help if we prayed for rain?). The dry air is harsh and the light unvarying, all days and all times of day are much alike. It is public weather, weather for processions, not for private living, and we long for our intimate island summer, for the soft freshness and the silvery light, for our filtered sunshine and changing clouds and the shining fall of rain from skies brimming with showers like eyes with tears.

> "O Western wind when wilt thou blow,
> That the small rain down may rain?"

It is a cry of longing from an Englishman in a continental summer, thirsting in the heat and dust and metallic light for the misty small rain blowing in from the western seas.

For the West wind has a curious quality of enclosing and making private. Other winds clear the air and lay open the landscape, but the West wind softens the light and blurs all edges, enveloping us in gentle walls of moving air. It is a secret and intimate wind, for intimate love-affairs, and the poet's second longing is one with the first.

"O Western wind when wilt thou blow,
That the small rain down may rain?
Christ that my love were in my arms
And I in my bed again."

But today's wind blows from the south and we sit in the window. Above the trees in the hollow of the valley a flock of rooks rises and falls on the wind like blown leaves, like huge black insects. There is thunder somewhere high up beyond the scudding clouds, but casual, incidental, a distant commotion which does not concern us, with none of the drama of the brooding self-intent thunder-storms of hot windless weather. The jackdaws feeding in a scattered flock on the other side of the valley gather together in a close dark group in the middle of the field and wait uneasily. For the rain is coming: the distant hills are blurred already, and the grey-falling showers move in a swaying curtain towards us across the valley.

And now the first cloud has reached us, trailing rain like a jellyfish trailing tentacles. The drops spatter on the window, and the landscape through the glass is suddenly crooked with silvery angles of broken light. It is colder: we are glad of our push-button fire. Here inside we are sheltered completely, we can watch the storm with insulating glass between us, can sit and read in luxurious comfort, and later on draw the curtains and enclose our warm and lamplit cell against the dark.

Supper, and the night rattles with hail against the windows. We carry our coffee back to comfortable chairs, and the house is a boat in the stormy ocean of night which flows wild all round us. But in this room it is peaceful; reality for us is this warm and still and lamplit space, and the storm beyond our boundaries only invades our calm when we choose to listen. We read in silence (I have given up *Crime and Punishment* for *The Portrait of a Lady*), while the wind roars under the eaves and the rain breaks in waves against the window.

It is nine o'clock. Ten. William sits dark against the white wall with his hands in his trouser pockets and his open book bright on his knees. Is it only the shine from the light on his hair, or is he paling to silver on the temples? It is very distinguished: it will suit him to go grey. Feeling me watch him he looks up and smiles without speaking.

The wind is calmer now under the eaves and the rain taps gently against the window. The quiet house is benign and life-enhancing. Yet our lives here are much as they always are: we read the same books, listen to the same music; our only half-articulate converse of a long-married couple is indistinguishable here or in London. It is the quality of the living which is changed, and for William even more than for me, since I make my own emotional climate by my own intensities. But for William life here is on a different level of experience, and the everyday business of living is enhanced to conscious pleasure, like words sung to music.

Benefits given and received are the natural traffic of affection, and with those we love we are seldom surprised into conscious gratitude. But for this house in the country which now means so much to him William is grateful, as I am grateful to William always for the wind he blows in my sails.

◇◇◇◇◇ 32 ◇◇◇◇◇

"If you don't stop gardening soon you'll have nothing left for next summer."

The boys' tone is teasing but their intention is serious, for since they came back from the sea and William went back to

London we have worked steadily and non-stop at making a garden. Or rather I have worked non-stop and the boys have worked stop and start, and now they want no more starting.

"What will you do if you've nothing left? Just *think* how bored you'd be. You'd really better save some of the garden for another year." Certainly they intend to do no more themselves this holiday: I recognize the decision behind the banter. "We'll be glad to get back to school again you know, and have a rest."

They watch me cautiously, unsure of my reaction. They are half-wary, half-amused, but with an underlying air of being determined to weather all storms.

It is the revolt I have been expecting all summer, for they have already done far more work in the garden than I ever dreamt they would. No one can enjoy the hard labour in somebody else's garden. It is tedious enough for the gardener in pursuit of his vision, and the boys are not gardeners at all, but adolescents who will soon leave home for lives which have nothing to do with this house. It is not their garden, they are not interested. I have merely channelled off some of their surplus energy and diverted it into mowing grass and moving soil instead of riding bicycles and swimming. And they have been wonderfully good-natured about it, offering themselves like animals for labour in an irresponsible cheerful way.

But as a precedent for future holidays they are understandably less enthusiastic about the arrangement. Clearly they have thought it over: they have decided they must have it out with me. The day has come and they have taken me aside. Now that they have reached the crucial moment they are very serious and very reasonable.

"We'll still go on helping you" (they must have agreed beforehand what they would say, for they stand together solemnly united). "We'll go on helping you in the holidays, but we don't want to help every holiday, and not all the time. What we want is to have definite jobs to do, so that we know what they are. Then we can do them when we feel like it and be finished. What we don't like is how it's been this summer."

I listen and say nothing, trying to reconstruct the committee meeting which must have preceded this united show of sweet reason. Did they get together in disgruntled irritation I wonder, and vent their feelings by planning revolt? Did they hold forth to each other in furious relieving chorus against my slave-driving methods? If so it is all over. No one could be milder or friendlier (or more determined), and I am amused to be dealt with so exactly in my own terms, recognizing in their voices the same note of deliberately reasonable persuasion which they must have heard a hundred times in mine.

For weeks now I have been waiting for the well-justified rebellion, but expecting some sudden goaded outburst with tempers flying on both sides, and the rest of the holidays airy defiance. Certainly I never imagined any constructive offers of long-term help. Nor did they, it seems, imagine that I should accept their default so meekly. In fact we are all surprised by how well we are all behaving.

I think most parents realize the difficulties of adolescents in the unnatural position of children, but few adolescents realize the equally unnatural position of parents responsible for adolescents. I doubt whether these two are conscious of anything so complicated: they are only friendly and carefully fair. And since each side is so much more reasonable than the other expected, we are quickly and happily agreed. The arrangement is simple and definite: they will help in the garden with anything I like for two weeks a year: a week at Easter and a week at the end of the summer holidays. But if they do anything in between it will only be as a favour because they feel like it, or in exchange for something special I do for them.

We are all agreed and all delighted. It is more than I hoped and less than they feared: the ideal overlap. Certainly I can see that the first few years will need rather many favours from them and special services from me, and also that I shall have to put in a depressing amount of hard work by myself to make up the extra, but never mind. I have my two weeks promised.

Meanwhile the recently overcast family weather has cleared to a sunny calm as peaceful as the September days on this quiet hill-side. The boys go off swimming in the neighbouring reservoir with no sense of guilt, and I watch them go without irritation, for we now know where we are in this question of holiday jobs. It is this matter-of-fact disposing of emotional situations which makes these half-grown boys so simple to live with. And because they now feel it a favour and not an unwilling duty (for we agreed that they owed not a second's more work till next Easter), they come out unasked and help me for odd half-hours with a cheerful energy which makes even gardening a larky pastime.

September is one of the year's transitions, a month which begins in summer and ends in autumn. And in our lives too there is a change of season, less violent but just as definite as the yearly upheaval of spring: it is the autumn emotional migration from one way of living to another. In most years it happens towards the end of September and it is happening to us now. The week is still undisturbed, the same camping-out summer life on this tranquil hill-side, but the week-ends begin to be restless. We begin to be troubled by the consciousness of London, by William on Friday night brimming with the week's news, and friends on Sunday visiting us from their urban world.

There is one particular Sunday evening when the last car carries the last waving children and their parents up the drive and away, and I realize that the season has changed. All August it was we who were the fortunate ones, and stayed in Arcadia when the rest must go back to the city. All August the leavers looked back longingly as we waved them off from our evening hill-side and settled contentedly back again to the country life.

But surely today they leave us more cheerfully, surely they look back less lingeringly and drive off faster down the lane towards London?

Or do I only imagine? Am I the only one who has changed? Certainly tonight I no longer turn back readily from their departure to our interrupted life. Now that they have gone there is a twinge, still faint, but undeniable, at being left behind. And when William goes too it is not a twinge at all, but a dreadful wrench, a wave of forsakenness which sweeps back over me from the wake of his disappearing car.

The hill-side is deserted now, the sun shines less warmly, and surely the evening air smells of winter approaching. The rooms are empty, where friends all day have lolled and talked and strolled in and out from the terrace: not empty and peaceful as they were in the evenings of early summer, but empty and forlorn. And the friends are speeding back to London, to the swift and companionable and close-packed and exhilarating urban life which I left, how many lifetimes ago? Not since the war years of exile have I ever been so long away from the city, for I am a Londoner by whole-hearted adoption, even though the sound of Bow Bells never reached within miles of my northern cradle. In an absence of more than a week or two the longing to be back in the atmosphere of a metropolis is a steadily worsening homesickness which brings me hurrying back from even the most idyllic of holidays. It is a measure of the upheaval in my life that in the last three summers I have forgotten our London life for months together.

But now I remember. Now the homesickness is beginning. This is not where I live, in this quiet green valley: this is the country I delight in as contrast, as change from our life of city streets. And I want to go back. I want the opposite houses close across the street, not this wide sweep of valley outside the windows. I want pavements alive with people, not empty fields. I want the traffic and the shops and the speed and the various life and the impersonal companionableness of a city. I long for London.

And even more intimately I long for the lost familiar routine of our so-much-distracted family life. I want to get up to our London working-day mornings, with the boys off early to school, and William and I reading out snippets to each other from the morning papers over our breakfast coffee before he leaves for the hospital. I want the regularly assembled family evening meal, with the table laid, and properly cooked food on properly washed plates. I want even the repetitive domestic routine of shopping and cooking and all the rest.

Suddenly I am overwhelmed by a huge wave of boredom which has gathered unnoticed through these last years of make-shift family living. I am suddenly and excruciatingly bored with make-shift, bored with the raw, the unfinished, the hurried, the disrupted, the domestically draughty; all the sense of making-do which has pervaded our family life since we started the house. The boys have revolted and so do I. If William were not half an hour's driving out of earshot I would run after his London-bound car and leave all this behind me. I want no more of it. It is suddenly intolerable to spend another single day in this cut-off existence. We are missing too much. The sun may still shine on our valley but it shines as brilliantly on the busy London streets. Our real life is not here and I want to go home.

What are their plans for the rest of the holidays? I ask the boys tentatively as we sit round the kitchen table and they finish off a box of peppermint creams left them by our vanished visitors.

Yes, they say eagerly. That's just what they wanted to ask me. When are we going back to London?

They are as unsettled as I am, it seems, by the sudden consciousness of life going on without them thirty-five miles away. For the talk today has been London talk, and our visitors leaving has set up a suction which draws us after them back to the city. (I wonder if migrating swallows ever carry other birds with them when they leave.)

"When would you like to go?" I ask the boys, carefully non-committal.

"As soon as we can. Straight away. We've got crowds and crowds of things we want to do in London before school starts."

"Alright," I agree. "We'll go when you like."

"Splendid. Let's go tomorrow."

But not quite tomorrow. Nor even the next day. It is not that I am any less eager to be off than they are. Not at all: I am only longer-sighted. For this is an important stage in our occupation. If the house from now on is to count as finished, and our visits are no longer to be active sessions of work in progress as they have been till now, but leisured week-end visits to our house in the country—if from now on we are to live in so different and desirable a fashion, then there is still an unavoidable amount of finishing-off to do before we leave. There are still a hundred odd things to do in the house, put off till now from day to day because the sun shone and the garden was more inviting. There are curtains still to hem and furniture to paint, cushions to cover, hooks to put up, cupboards to rearrange, mirrors to hang, plugs still to rewire—all the myriad minor makeshifts of a newly inhabited house. And the garden too. If it is to look after itself till next Easter, then it must be prepared for the winter and not simply left. The grass must be finally mown and raked, the weeds cut down and burnt.

But through it all now, London is a carrot which dangles before all our eager noses. With no word of persuasion from me the boys offer themselves for work after breakfast. The sooner we finish the sooner we shall be off: there is no need to say it. They have never made so light of garden labour. While I dispose of the household jobs full-speed indoors they walk round non-stop behind the grass-cutter singing at the top of their voices. We have never been so gay, never so delighted with each other. It is as if we were all playing truant together and escaping to a London life of enticing holiday.

Whatever the changes are that cause the autumn migration they have certainly happened to us. We came out here for the summer—it was Arcady then and Eden, and nowhere in the world more delightful. But now the summer is over, and we want to go back to London.

◇◇◇◇ 33 ◇◇◇◇

William is amused but not surprised when we arrive back a week before we intended, and even to me our would-be plausible reasons for needing to be back in town sound much less convincing than our obvious delight in simply being here. Besides, this is only our usual early return home from pleasures abroad when the idea of coming back once invades our holiday consciousness. It is a form of impatience, of liking things done as soon as thought of, a taste for experience early in the season.

So back we now are, and with order reassuringly achieved in the country behind us. Already the boys have gone off round the town on their city concerns, disappearing into the vast busy sea of London like fish back in water, and coming home only for meals and sleep. And I too have surveyed and reoccupied our London territory, reregistered the different rooms of the house like a cat, done a quick round of the streets and shops to re-establish the urban setting of our family life, and rung up surrounding friends to greet them. For though they have been out to see us on summer Sundays, the country-dwellers they visited and left behind them were not our present city-centred selves. We greet them now as Londoners, as one of their number.

Living. *In*

Even in these first few days the metropolitan air is already newly familiar again after absence. I am home again, but still it is strange to be back, as if I had returned from an exile I never realized while it lasted. As indeed I have in consciousness if not in fact, for though in these last years I have spent more time in London than not, I have only been physically here, it is not what I now remember. I have met my friends no doubt, but forgotten the meetings. And since our domestic life runs much as it always did, I must have dealt with the household situations despite my abstraction. But I do not remember: the conscious centre of living has been miles away from my physical self.

It is as if our country and our London lives were two circles which partly overlap like a partial eclipse, and since the new house started I had only inhabited the small section of the London circle covered by the country one. But now I am back on the London side and living is reorientated on the town. It is the country now which we shall inhabit only in city terms of week-end leisure. For this is a true return, not simply one more distracted interval between sessions of house-making.

It is a home-coming which the family seem to recognize as clearly as I do, and they greet me with amusement as if I were back from a journey. As indeed I am, from a two-and-a-half-year preoccupation, and never more content to be home again, whether early or late. For now that the wind of activity is sinking, I begin to realize all that has had to be pushed aside in the doing, all the pleasant pattern of family living disturbed, the leisure and intimacies crowded out. Another year and I might almost have forgotten how delightful the family are as companions as distinct from responsibilities: my dearest and closest friends neglected and all for a house. It is as if I were recovering from partial amnesia and returning to a half-forgotten life.

But now we are back together, a London family reunited, and in celebration I have filled the house with flowers—urban flowers now, no more buttercups and daisies—long-stemmed roses and the first purple anemones on our dressing-table and fat brown chrysanthemums so exactly like opulent city men that I always expect them to smell of cigars. It is a glorious flowery extravagance, justified (so I assure myself) by all the jobs I have done in the house myself instead of having the workmen. And for celebration supper we will have roast duck with trimmings for poor gourmet William so long fobbed off with five-minute omelettes.

But he shall be no longer: from now on I will cook for and cosset him. Not that he has minded the long upheaval, being undomestic and easily comfortable. I have minded far more than he has, and now at last there is time for our life together again: time to plan and savour and be peaceful. Private evenings at home, sociable evenings with friends, all the pleasures that London offers for the winter season—there will be time now for everything. I can make up at last the long arrears of civilized living. For makers have bouts of making with pauses between, and I only hope this pause is a long one. I want people now, not houses, for the bouts are a lonely business, and even with the companions around us we are too preoccupied for any real contact. So now I want people: William first, then the boys, but my friends too and our family friends, acquaintances, strangers— widening circles of people all with their sociable concerns.

And now for the first time in years I can sit in a chair again and cross my legs and happily do nothing. For leisure is an attitude of mind, not simply remission of work. As for that there is plenty to do, but the housekeeping here is a settled routine of work and needs no conscious attention. It can be planned and fitted into the week to leave time for leisure, and that is an altogether different matter from living surrounded by an inexhaustible supply of tasks waiting to be done. Like the boys I am glad to be back for a rest. And since in these last crowded years I have organized the housekeeping to run perfectly well with my part-time efforts, I now have no intention

of letting it fill the whole of the week. From now on I shall
keep time for living-in. I shall be idle now and waste time if I
want to. I shall get up in the mornings in nylon stockings not
working jeans, and I shall go through my wardrobe (that much-
neglected entity) and rearrange my clothes for an urban winter.

For the new house is safely accomplished. Certainly it still
needs months of finishing-off, but with so much achieved the
rest can wait till some later-on of revived enthusiasm. So can the
garden. It is safely subdued for the next six months and can
come to no harm. I shall forget it for the winter, and when the
sun shines warm next spring I shall no doubt be eager to start
again.

Or so I suppose. But to my re-emerged urban self it seems as
unlikely as wanting to swim in the North Sea in mid-winter.
Just now I can't imagine ever willingly doing anything else at all
in either garden or house. If I run and rest, then this is rest. Very
definitely rest.

The house is already separate: an undertaking completed. Its
creation belongs to a different phase of existence, which is over
now and part of the swiftly receding past. We have paid for it
not only with the Regency Villa but also with two and a half
years of my preoccupation, and now that it is safely achieved
what matters most is our lives together, the reaffirming of our
particular synthesis of the stuff of living which the house is built
to hold.

In these last years I have done a most uncivilized amount of
work, and I look back with horror now at what I took on so
gaily. Shall I always be in danger, I wonder, of setting off
blindly on such undertakings? And if I had had any idea before I
began of the exhaustions ahead, should I ever have started? And
would I do it again? No. Certainly not.

But perhaps I would, for the effort will soon be forgotten
and the house is such lasting treasure. Treasure for William
above all else, for already he so delights in it that no effort is too

high a price. Of all the rewards this is the most satisfactory: that William so loves his new house that he quite simply goes there whenever he can. No matter what the hour or the weather, he drives out unconcerned by storms or forecast of storms, arrives with the same content at mid-night as mid-morning. The house is now the setting of a world he inhabits with profound and increasing satisfaction. It is enough only to be there, a pleasure positive in itself, as if the walls enclosed not simply a space for living in but a whole different way of living, concentrated and made accessible in solid bricks and mortar.

There will never be any question now about being safely rooted, for William's strongly growing enthusiasm will put down an anchoring tap-root for all of us. We have a family base now for the years ahead—for generations ahead perhaps, though there is no way of knowing what the children will want of their lives. But certainly the house is there for us, even though for years yet we shall be absorbed in other interests, being still in full flood of our working lives. And just as the inanimate house will draw life not only from our present leisure but also from the promise of our future occupation, so too it will enhance our human lives by drawing together into a single whole the different parts which would otherwise be separate and self-limited. Middle-age and old-age, work and leisure, our lives and the children's—linked together by the house they are more than the sum of their different parts because they give depth to each other.

In its green valley the house stands remote and serene, and to remember it now in London is not merely to confirm a material fact, it is like remembering a dream of reality made vivid by the visionary light. For the unpredictable transformation has happened, and our new house is a swan unmistakably.

"The Corn was Orient and Immortal Wheat, which never should be reaped, nor was ever sown. I thought it had stood from everlasting to everlasting."

Living. *In*

Traherne's wheat grew in his boyhood fields and ours is last year's sowing, but nonetheless it is corn of the same precious species. For it is not distance but the climate it grows in which transforms mere grain to golden treasure. No matter when we plant it, most of our harvest is never more than corn for the millers, and only a small proportion ever grows to the Orient Wheat that stands everlastingly in our memories. But the proportion grows gold now as then, and we still come on fields which will never be reaped. But neither can they ever be sown with certainty: we can only plant our seed-corn and wait to see whether the light will shine on its growing. And on our new house it shines already: for us its plain bricks already glow with the proper visionary radiance. So the long earthquake is over at last and the troubled ground has brought forth its harvest—the unpredictable, mysterious, imperishable, life-sustaining, ever-to-be-hoped-for, authentic Orient Wheat.

A NOTE ON THE TYPE

The text of this book was set on the Linotype in
Janson, a recutting made direct from the type cast
from matrices long thought to have been made by
Anton Janson, a Dutchman who was a practising
type-founder in Leipzig during the years 1668–
1687. However, it has been conclusively demon-
strated that these types are actually the work of
Nicholas Kis (1650–1702), a Hungarian who
learned his trade most probably from the master
Dutch type-founder Dirk Voskens.

The type is an excellent example of the influential
and sturdy Dutch types that prevailed in England
prior to the development by William Caslon
(1692–1766) of his own incomparable designs,
which he evolved from these Dutch faces. The
Dutch in their turn had been influenced by Claude
Garamond (1510–1561) in France. The general
tone of the Janson, however, is darker than Garamond and has a sturdiness and substance quite different from its predecessors.

This book was composed, printed, and bound by
THE HADDON CRAFTSMEN, INC., SCRANTON, PA. Typog-
raphy and binding based on designs by HARRY FORD.